P9-CBU-417

GREAT AMERICAN ROAD TRIPS
National Parks

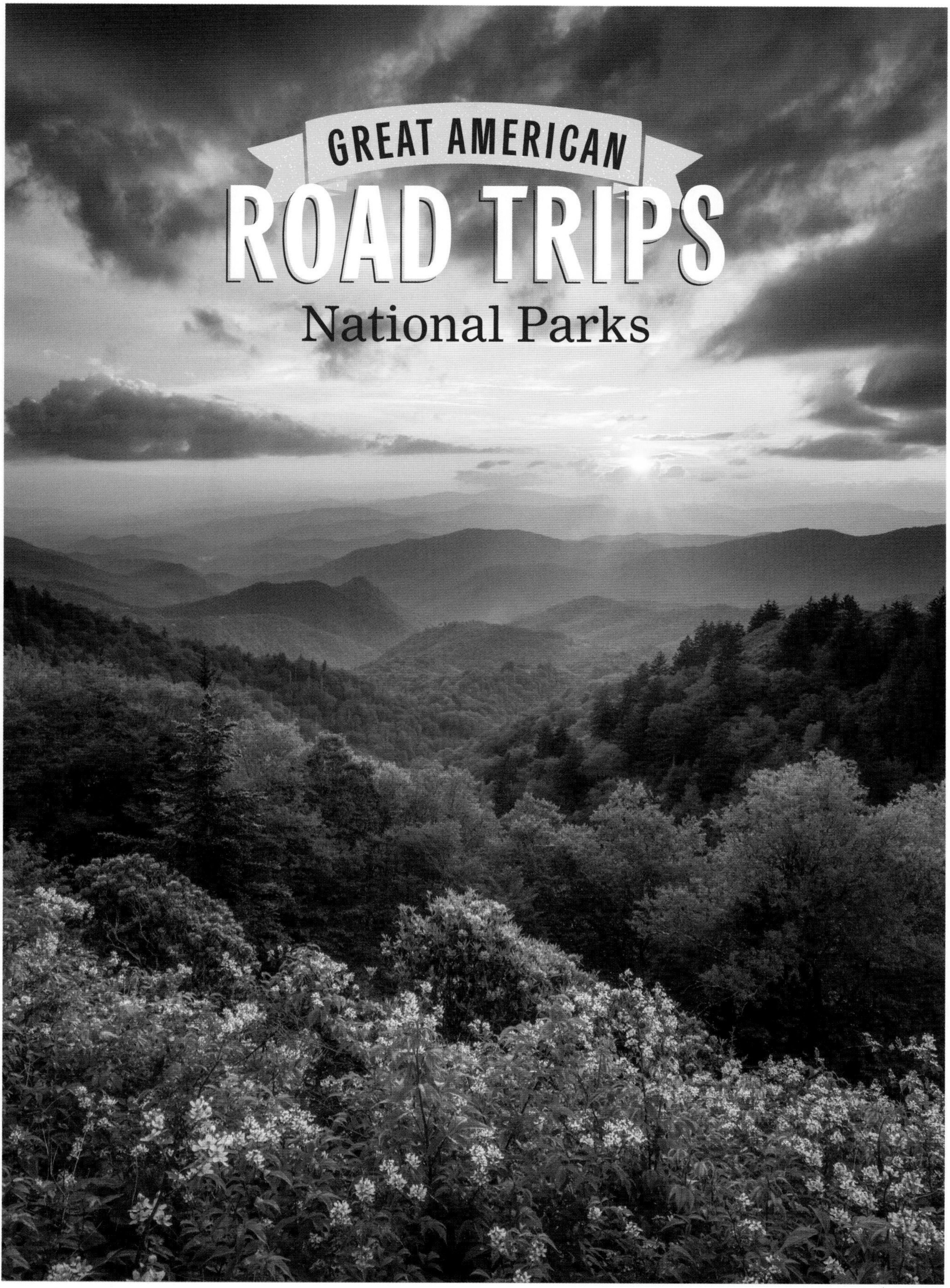

▼
Great Smoky Mountains National Park and its spring rhododendron and blackberry blooms.

▼
Birds on the beach in Cape Canaveral.

PICTURED ON FRONT COVER
Wotans Throne at Cape Royal on the North Rim in Grand Canyon National Park, Arizona, by Tim Fitzharris

ILLUSTRATIONS Anna Simmons

ADDITIONAL PHOTO INFORMATION
Pages 8-9: 1916: Library of Congress/Getty Images; 1927: Trigger Image/Alamy Stock Photo; 1933: Everett Collection Inc/Alamy Stock Photo; 1935: Charles Johnson/Getty Images; 1958: John Springer Collection/Getty Images; 1968 (Shoshone Falls, Idaho): muddymari/Getty Images; 1968 (Glacier Point, Yosemite): Smith Collection/Getty Images; 1994: benedek/Getty Images; 1995: Steve McKinzie/Getty Images; 2015: Arterra/Getty Images; 2016: Robert Alexander/Getty Images
Page 10: Cathedral Spires, Yosemite National Park, California, by Tim Fitzharris
Page 94: Balanced Rock, Big Bend National Park, Texas, by Tim Fitzharris
Page 118: Petit Portal arch, Pictured Rocks National Lakeshore, Michigan, by John McCormick
Page 152: Bass Harbor Head Light Station, Acadia National Park, Maine, by Ultima_Gaina/Getty Images

© 2021 RDA Enthusiast Brands, LLC.
1610 N. 2nd St., Suite 102
Milwaukee, WI 53212-3906

INTERNATIONAL STANDARD BOOK NUMBER
978-1-62145-729-9 (Hardcover)
978-1-62145-730-5 (Paperback)

LIBRARY OF CONGRESS CONTROL NUMBER
2020950715

COMPONENT NUMBER
116500102H

All rights reserved.
Printed in China.
1 3 5 7 9 10 8 6 4 2
(Hardcover)
1 3 5 7 9 10 8 6 4 2
(Paperback)

CONTENTS

WEST

SOUTHWEST

MIDWEST

EAST

Joshua Tree National Park is an incredible place to watch golden sunsets.

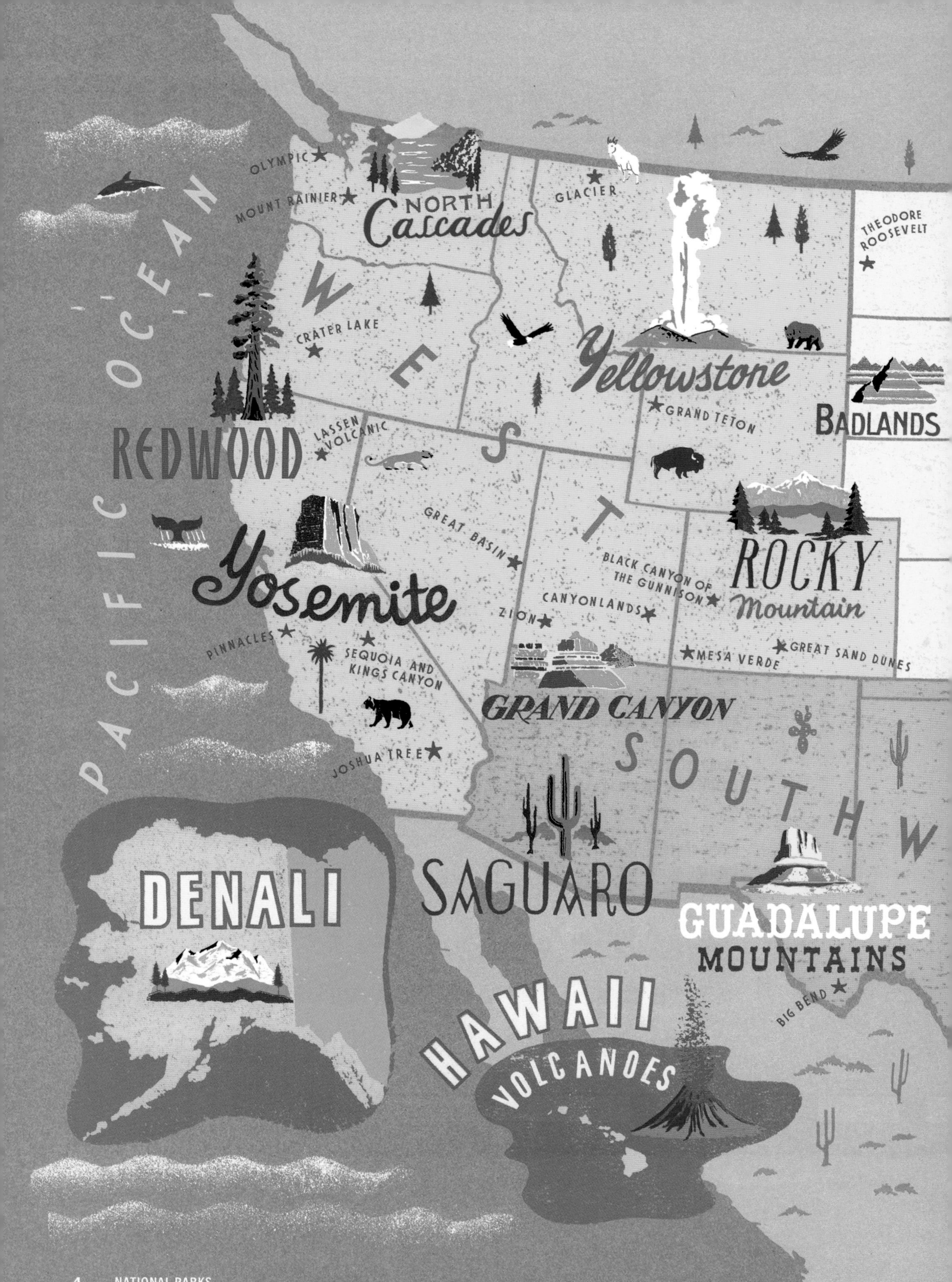
PACIFIC OCEAN
OLYMPIC
MOUNT RAINIER
NORTH
Cascades
GLACIER
THEODORE ROOSEVELT
WEST
CRATER LAKE
Yellowstone
GRAND TETON
BADLANDS
REDWOOD
LASSEN VOLCANIC
ROCKY
Mountain
GREAT BASIN
BLACK CANYON OF THE GUNNISON
CANYONLANDS
ZION
Yosemite
PINNACLES
SEQUOIA AND KINGS CANYON
MESA VERDE
GREAT SAND DUNES
GRAND CANYON
JOSHUA TREE
SOUTHW
SAGUARO
DENALI
GUADALUPE
MOUNTAINS
BIG BEND
HAWAII
VOLCANOES

ISLE ROYALE
SLEEPING BEAR Dunes
PICTURED ROCKS
APOSTLE ISLANDS
Acadia
Indiana Dunes
MIDWEST
SHENANDOAH
MAMMOTH CAVE
GREAT Smoky MOUNTAINS
CONGAREE
HOT SPRINGS
EAST
EST
ATLANTIC OCEAN
CANAVERAL
VIRGIN ISLANDS
EVERGLADES

MAJESTY PRESERVED

THE NEXT TIME you gaze into a stunning canyon stretching to the horizon, think of our personal freedoms. When you stare incredulously at a towering mountain range, consider the rich benefits of our democratic republic, and know that conserving land for the public's enrichment was a uniquely American idea at the start. The terrific momentum generated by Theodore and Franklin Delano Roosevelt to expand parklands in the early decades of the 20th century was unprecedented.

With minimal presidential power for such conservationist action at the time, only four national parks existed when Theodore became president in 1901—but landmark action was just over the horizon. By the time he left office in 1909, Americans enjoyed four more national parks, 18 national monuments, 51 federal bird sanctuaries, four national game preserves and 150 national forests, totaling 230 million acres of additional land set aside for public use.

Following his cousin's trailblazing, FDR improved parks while easing unemployment when he was president. As part of his New Deal relief program, FDR authorized the formation of the military-style Civilian Conservation Corps. Enrollees based in state and national parks advanced the conservation cause by reforesting land, fighting forest fires, creating or improving hiking trails, constructing fire lookout towers, building or restoring park lodges and more. In addition, FDR's Works Progress Administration employed artists from 1938 to 1941 to create eye-catching promotional posters for the parks. FDR not only added Olympic and Kings Canyon to the national parks list but also put many national monuments and all historic military sites under the umbrella of the National Park Service.

Other figures in American history helped maintain, grow and preserve the parks as well. John Muir is often called "father of the National Park System"

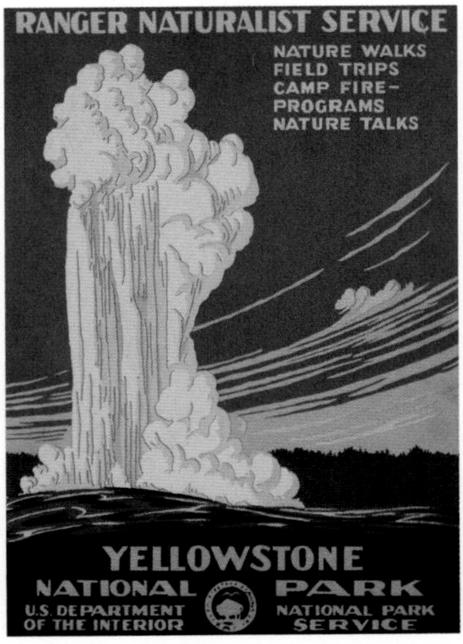

Posters created in the 1930s by the Works Progress Administration to promote the parks.

because of his advocacy for nature and his impassioned writings, which played an essential role in the establishment of Yosemite National Park, as well as the lands that would one day become Grand Canyon, Sequoia, Mount Rainier and Petrified Forest national parks.

Stephen T. Mather played an integral role in a key component of our parks: the National Park Service. Mather convinced Congress of the need for a National Park Service, and, in 1917, he became its first director. During his 12-year tenure, Shenandoah, Great Smoky Mountains and Mammoth Cave were added to the list of America's glorious protected lands.

New parks were added throughout the 20th century, with the aim of preserving nature, the land it calls home and the history contained within it. Michigan's Pictured Rocks became the country's first national lakeshore in 1966; California's Redwood, which houses the tallest trees on Earth, earned its national park designation two years later. And the number climbs still. With the addition of New River Gorge National Park in January 2021, awe-inspiring lands continue to be set aside for the appreciation and inspiration of future generations.

Our parks have proven instrumental in the protection of endangered and threatened species as well. Yellowstone played a key role in bolstering the populations of the American bison and gray wolf. Both species faced extreme challenges to their survival, but protection efforts at Yellowstone have allowed these animals a safe place to roam. Today, our parks are home to more than a thousand endangered or otherwise at-risk plants and animals, and they provide them a haven free from unlimited human interference.

Our national parks attracted more than 300 million visitors in 2019. Altogether, these travelers spent more than 1 billion hours hiking, biking, canoeing, sightseeing and more.

With this book, our wish is to provide a unique guide to these freedom-filled lands and emphasize why they're so special. Nature has risen recently on the list of popular American pastimes, but whether you're planning a trip or vacationing in your armchair, you'll enjoy fascinating stories and photos submitted by *Country* readers that speak to the majesty of these lands and their continued appeal.

We're excited that you're venturing into the glorious American wilderness with us, and we hope this book inspires you to treasure and explore these wondrous places in our country.

—EDITORS OF ***COUNTRY***

Top: Conservationist John Muir, right, with President Theodore Roosevelt at Glacier Point, Yosemite National Park, in 1906. Bottom: President Franklin D. Roosevelt visits a Civilian Conservation Corps camp.

THE PARKS THROUGH THE YEARS

1872

Yellowstone becomes the first national park in the U.S. and the world.

1890
SEQUOIA
CALIFORNIA

YOSEMITE
CALIFORNIA

1899
MOUNT RAINIER
WASHINGTON

1902
CRATER LAKE
OREGON

1906
MESA VERDE
COLORADO

1910
GLACIER
MONTANA

1913

Walter Harper, Harry Karstens, Hudson Stuck and Robert Tatum reach the summit of Denali in Alaska.

1915
ROCKY MOUNTAIN
COLORADO

1916

National Park Service is created to protect the parks. Stephen Mather becomes the first director in 1917.

1916
HAWAII VOLCANOES
HAWAII

LASSEN VOLCANIC
CALIFORNIA

1920

The number of total annual park visits exceeds 1 million.

1917
MOUNT McKINLEY (DENALI)
ALASKA

1958

Alfred Hitchcock and the cast of *North by Northwest* arrive to film scenes at Mount Rushmore. When the park service revokes their permit, they shoot the chase scene using a replica.

1960

Yellowstone starts a strict bear management program.

1964
CANYONLANDS
UTAH

1966

Michigan's Pictured Rocks becomes the first national lakeshore.

1968
NORTH CASCADES
WASHINGTON

REDWOOD
CALIFORNIA

1968

President Lyndon Johnson signs the Wild and Scenic Rivers Act to preserve certain rivers throughout the United States.

1968

The manmade Firefall events, during which burning embers were dropped from the top of Glacier Point in Yosemite, are stopped.

1970
APOSTLE ISLANDS
WISCONSIN

SLEEPING BEAR DUNES
MICHIGAN

1972
GUADALUPE MOUNTAINS
TEXAS

1973

President Richard Nixon signs the Endangered Species Act.

1975
CANAVERAL
FLORIDA

1978
BADLANDS
SOUTH DAKOTA

THEODORE ROOSEVELT
NORTH DAKOTA

1986
GREAT BASIN
NEVADA

1994
JOSHUA TREE
CALIFORNIA

1994
SAGUARO
ARIZONA

1919
ACADIA
MAINE

GRAND CANYON
ARIZONA

ZION
UTAH

1921
HOT SPRINGS
ARKANSAS

1926

Congress authorizes the creation of Great Smoky Mountains National Park.

1927

Ansel Adams' photograph "Monolith Face of Half Dome" receives critical acclaim. His black-and-white prints of Yosemite make him and the park famous.

1928

Newlyweds Bessie and Glen Hyde disappear while rafting the Colorado River in Grand Canyon National Park. Their fate is a mystery to this day.

1929
GRAND TETON
WYOMING

1933

FDR creates the Civilian Conservation Corps, which built important infrastructure in the parks, including campsites, trails and roads.

1933

Historic sites come under jurisdiction of the National Parks Service.

1935
SHENANDOAH
VIRGINIA

1938
OLYMPIC
WASHINGTON

1940
ISLE ROYALE
MICHIGAN

KINGS CANYON
CALIFORNIA

1941

Ansel Adams is hired to photograph the national parks.

1941
MAMMOTH CAVE
KENTUCKY

1942

WWII reduces the number of visitors by 11.5 million.

1944
BIG BEND
TEXAS

1947
EVERGLADES
FLORIDA

1956
VIRGIN ISLANDS
ST. JOHN

1995

Gray wolves from Western Canada are relocated to Yellowstone.

1999
BLACK CANYON OF THE GUNNISON
COLORADO

2003
CONGAREE
SOUTH CAROLINA

2004
GREAT SAND DUNES
COLORADO

2013
PINNACLES
CALIFORNIA

2015

Alaska's Mount McKinley is renamed Denali.

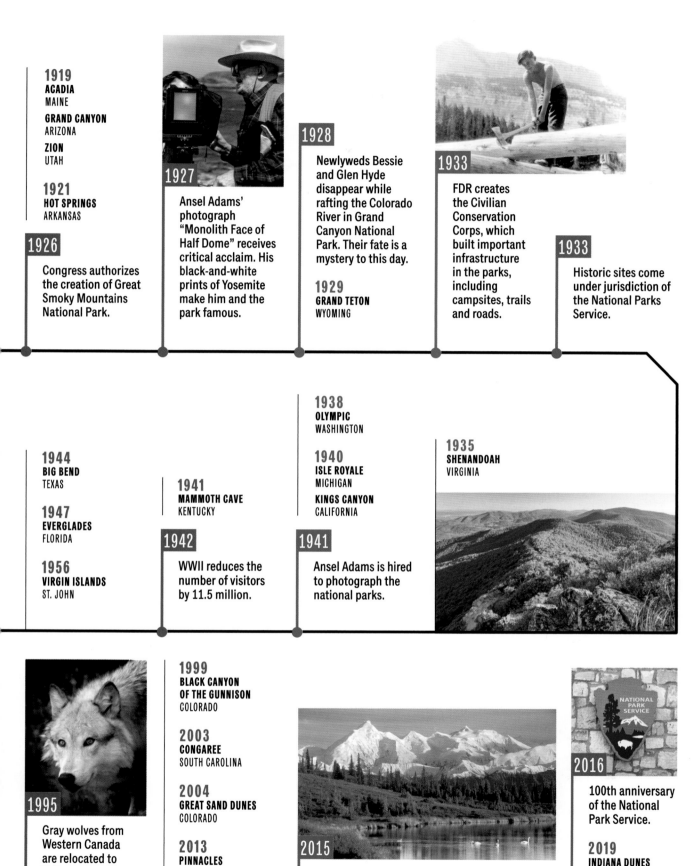

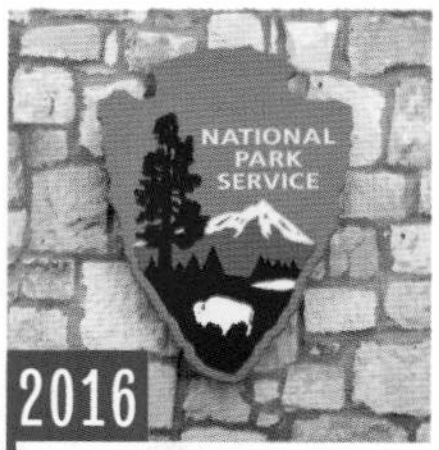

2016

100th anniversary of the National Park Service.

2019
INDIANA DUNES
INDIANA

WEST
REDWOODS · VOLCANOES · MOUNTAINS

▼
Quaking aspens welcome visitors to the Riley Creek Campground.

STORY AND PHOTOS BY
MICHAEL QUINTON

DENALI

SEE NATURE IN THE RAW ON THE ONLY ROAD THROUGH ALASKA'S FIRST NATIONAL PARK.

WHETHER YOU'RE NEGOTIATING the sharp switchbacks on Polychrome Pass or eagerly anticipating what surprises might lurk just around the bend, the Denali Park Road will keep you on the edge of your seat.

The 92-mile road is the only one through Alaska's Denali National Park and Preserve. It winds through diverse landscapes of spruce forests, braided riverbeds, alpine tundra and some of North America's most spectacular mountain vistas, including the country's highest peak. The 20,310-foot-high Denali (which means "the high one" in one of the Athabascan languages) is a hiker's and backpacker's paradise—but don't forget your bear spray.

The first 16 miles, to Savage River, are paved. After that, the road becomes well-maintained gravel. Generally, the road is open to travelers between mid-May and September and to dogsled teams in the winter. There are six campgrounds along the way. Three of them, Sanctuary River, Igloo Creek and Wonder Lake, are reserved for tent camping.

Visitors must walk, bike or take a bus tour beyond the Savage River Bridge unless they have a private vehicle road permit. As a professional wildlife photographer, I was one of the lucky few able to enter a public lottery for one of these coveted permits.

Road construction began in 1923, when crews blasted rock and moved gravel to create it. The road stretches from the park entrance to Kantishna Roadhouse, a back country lodge, and was finished in 1938. In the 1960s, plans were made to widen and pave

A candid moment between a grizzly bear sow and her cub.

FUN FACTS

Until 2015, the country's highest peak and the park's main attraction was officially called Mount McKinley, in honor of the President William McKinley, who was assassinated in 1901. In 2015, the mountain's name was reverted to its original Koyukon name, Denali, after a decades-long debate.

SIDE TRIP

After possibly returning from the Eielson Visitor Center (an 8-hour round-trip bus ride) or Wonder Lake (11 hours round-trip), resume the drive behind the wheel of your own vehicle. Grip it tight, though, because the next 65-mile stretch, which meets the scenic gorge of the Nenana River, is riddled with sharp turns, windy passes, canyon crossings and frost heaves. About 20 miles north of Nenana, the route reaches Skyline Drive, running along the ridgetops with spectacular views.

the road, but park officials opted to keep it and its surroundings as pristine as possible.

The park owes its creation to naturalist Charles Sheldon. During the winter of 1907-'08, Sheldon observed the slaughter of some 2,000 magnificent Dall sheep, killed by market hunters to be sold to railroad workers and gold miners. Realizing that this kind of pressure would quickly deplete the wild sheep herds, Sheldon joined with the Boone and Crockett Club, the country's oldest conservation group, and convinced Congress to protect this ecosystem.

In 1917, President Woodrow Wilson signed a bill establishing more than 2 million untouched acres along the Alaska Range as McKinley National Park. The park was enlarged to 6 million acres and renamed Denali National Park and Preserve in 1980.

Though originally established to protect Dall sheep, the national park status has benefited the entire Denali ecosystem. Herds of caribou and many smaller mammals (arctic ground squirrels, hoary marmots, snowshoe hares, wolverines, lynx, red fox and porcupines) await the watchful visitor. And the Denali Park Road is the best and safest place to view wolves and interior grizzly bears.

Birders will not be disappointed. Sightings of willow ptarmigan and golden eagles are guaranteed, but you might be lucky enough to see gyrfalcons, whimbrels, long-tailed jaegers, arctic warblers and rock and white-tailed ptarmigan.

Though Denali is in the heart of the Alaskan interior, wildlife is generally spread rather sparingly through it. But long summer days along the road offer many opportunities to witness nature in the raw. As dramatic as the landscapes are, I return to this mountain for those in-your-face encounters with wildlife.

The images often return to me. For example, one spring, a mama bear was snoozing on the open brown tundra. Nearby, a rufous-colored yearling cub lazily nipped grass shoots. Her brother, a straw blond, nosy cub, had become an annoyance to the females and was kept away. He entertained himself.

As I shot video of the bears, my son Josh observed a young black wolf approaching the bears.

After a brief stare, the wolf loped off toward the bears. The rufous cub was eager for confrontation. As the wolf circled, the cub pivoted and kept her big rear end pointing away from the wolf. The grizzly's short fuse smoldered; wolf's golden eyes burned; bear exploded. In perfect sync, the wolf whirled and moved on.

Then, slipping up close behind the big, sleepy sow, the brazen wolf pressed her nose into the sow's fur. The annoyed bear slowly rose, swung her huge head and eased into position. Like a lightning flash, a crushing hook ripped out a thick swath of…fresh mountain air.

Frustrated, the sow began to graze, shadowed by the wolf. When the sow bedded down again, the wolf made her move. In a playful pounce, she nipped the grizzly on the behind. Satisfied, her coup complete, the wolf trotted off down the road.

I wonder whether pushing the mama bear's buttons was just reckless fun or survival. Either way, for memories that truly last a lifetime, the Denali Park Road delivers.

The Denali Park Road is the best place to view wolves and bears.

STORY AND PHOTOS BY
LAURENCE PARENT

JOSHUA TREE

FIND OTHERWORLDLY BEAUTY WHERE THE COLORADO AND MOJAVE DESERTS MEET IN JOSHUA TREE NATIONAL PARK.

WHEN I TURN OFF Interstate 10 east of Palm Springs, California, the traffic fades and the road climbs north toward the wrinkled Cottonwood and Eagle mountains. The stark Colorado Desert surrounds me. The terrain is harsh and so rugged that hardy plants like creosote bush struggle to survive in the heat and dry air.

After turning onto Cottonwood Springs Road, I stop briefly at the Cottonwood Visitor Center to pick up information and stroll through the small man-made palm oasis. Birds twitter in the trees, attracted, like me, to the water and shade.

I continue my drive, eventually turning northwest onto Pinto Basin Road. I stop at a garden full of Bigelow cholla cacti. The thick golden spines catch my eye, but I approach the plants warily. Cholla segments break off easily when brushed by careless hikers, and their barbed spines cling to clothes and skin.

From the garden, I leave the Colorado Desert and drive higher into the slightly wetter and cooler Mojave Desert. Here Joshua trees, a type of yucca, appear, their many limbs reaching upward as high as 40 feet. In some areas, the trees grow thickly enough to create a surreal, sparse forest among the giant tumbled granite boulders that dot the landscape at White Tank, Jumbo Rocks and other areas.

I pause at the Ryan Ranch turnout and walk a short trail to explore ruins left behind by miners and ranchers who eked out a living in the park's rough country.

There are five fan palm oases in the park, and my next stop is the 49 Palms Oasis. I leave the park to get to the trailhead. It's a 3-mile-round-trip hike to this gift of shade tucked away in a hidden canyon.

As I climb the trail, I wonder whether my efforts will be rewarded. After half an hour, I spot palm trees and soon reach them and relax in the shade, listening to fronds rattle in the breeze. The hike and the trip was worthwhile. ■

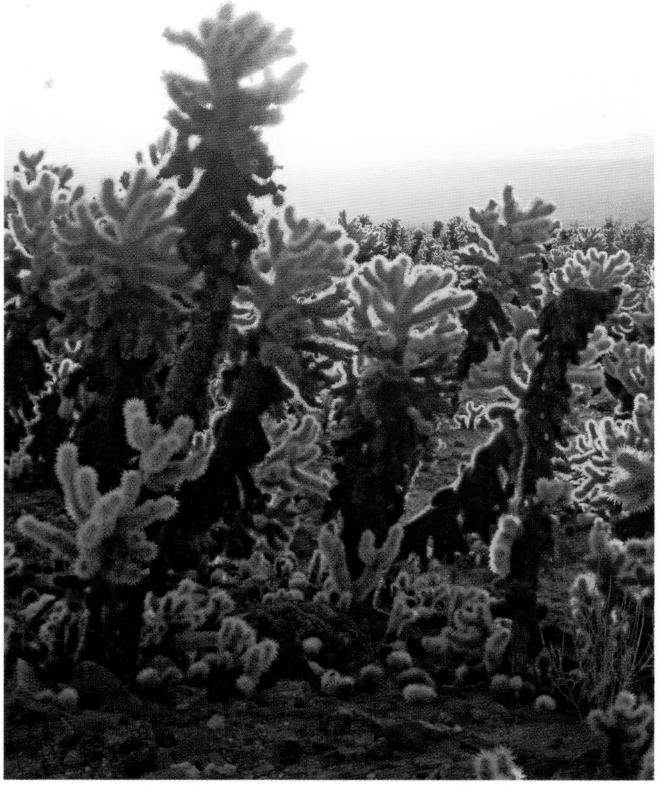

Top: The Joshua tree is a member of the agave family. Bottom: Beware of Bigelow cholla cacti!

POINTS OF INTEREST

NOT TO BE MISSED

Take in a beautiful view by following Keys View Road to the 5,000-foot-high overlook at Keys View. On a clear day you can see the San Jacinto Mountains and the Salton Sea.

WORDS TO THE WISE

Be on the alert for flash floods from thunderstorms.

SIDE TRIP

Just southwest of Joshua Tree National Park, drive part of the Palms to Pines Highway. Beginning at Palm Desert, the drive follows Routes 74 and 243 from palm-studded lowlands to the lofty pine woods of San Bernardino National Forest. At first, hairpin turns lead up the dizzying slopes of the Santa Rosa Mountains, followed by a smooth cruise through the grasslands of Garner Valley. Inviting trailheads await hikers at Idyllwild, and the last leg of the drive winds through the lushly forested San Jacinto Mountains, descending to the austere, boulder-strewn hills near Banning.

STORY BY
DANA MEREDITH

LASSEN VOLCANIC

EXPERIENCE GEOLOGICAL WONDERS WITHOUT THE CROWDS AT THIS UNDER-THE-RADAR SPOT THAT HAS ROOM TO ROAM.

FROM BUBBLING HYDROTHERMAL mud pots to one of the largest plug-dome volcanoes in the world, these 106,452 acres look like the setting for a sci-fi movie, but they make up Northern California's least-visited national park. The steep and winding 30-mile Lassen Volcanic National Park Highway transports you through dense forest from one amazing scenic overlook to the next (many with picnic areas and lakes). You'll see unbeatable views throughout the park from the comfort of your car.

But hop out and see geology in action on Bumpass Hell Trail, a moderate 3-mile hike—one option of 150 miles of trails that wind through forests and past lakes—to the largest hydrothermal area of the park.

Rise at dawn in one of the park's campgrounds or the rustic Drakesbad Guest Ranch, and hike the easy 1.5-mile Manzanita Lake Trail to catch sublime morning views of Lassen Peak. There is no motorized boating on the park's 20 lakes, but you can rent a canoe or a kayak for your exploring. If you're adventurous, hike up to the summit of Lassen Peak. Stops at the Kohm Yah-mah-nee Visitor Center and the Loomis Museum showcase the park's history and highlight the area's eruptions.

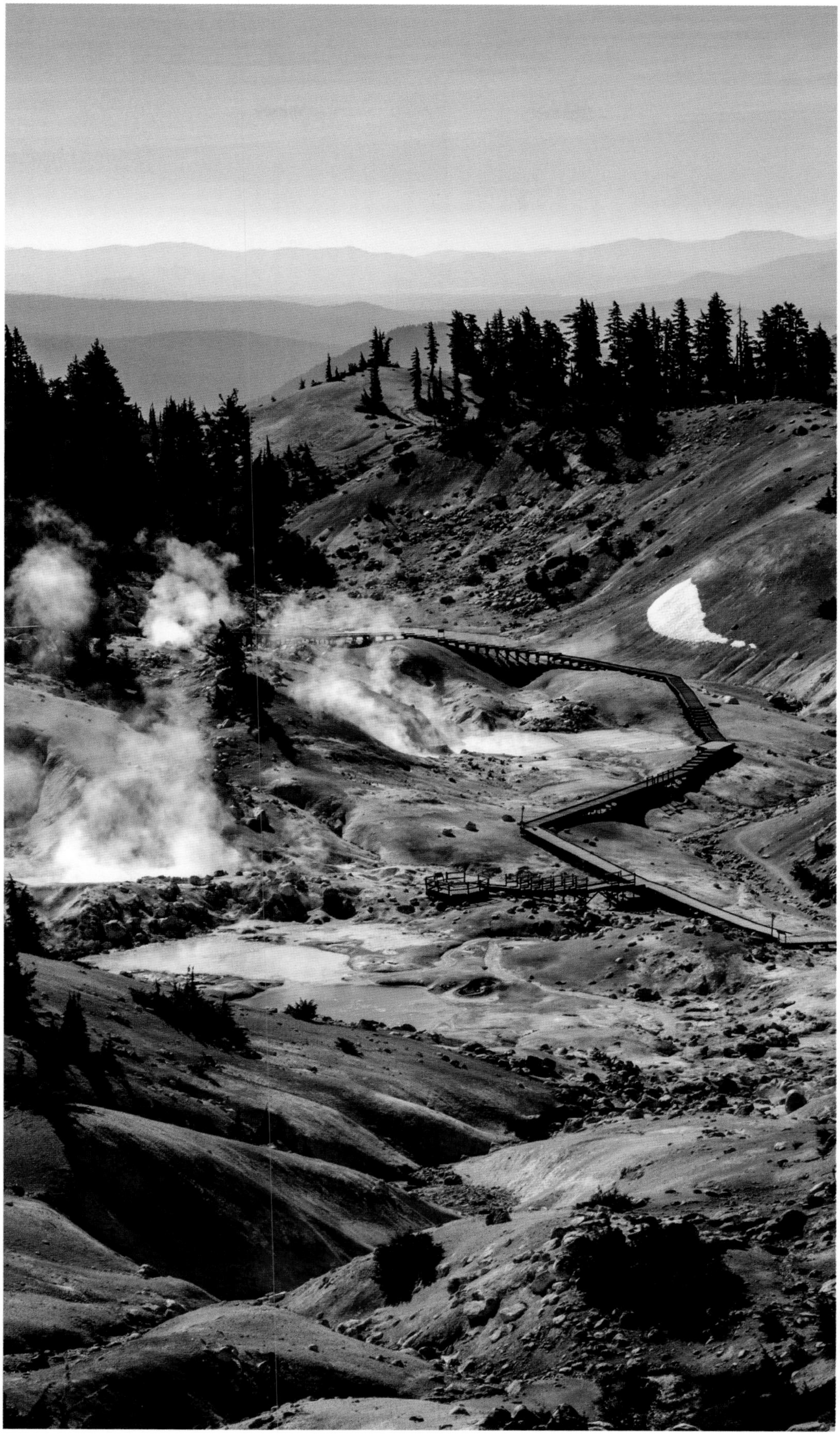

JOSHUA HAWLEY/GETTY IMAGES

Rising steam mists the air at the Bumpass Hell hydrothermal area.

POINTS OF INTEREST

NOT TO BE MISSED
The Lassen Dark Sky Festival, held annually in August, provides a fantastic opportunity to learn about the stars. If you are looking for the best views during the daytime, visit Bumpass Hell and Manzanita Lake.

FUN FACT
Lassen Peak last erupted for seven years beginning in 1914 and is the park's tallest volcano, at 10,457 feet.

WORDS TO THE WISE
Boardwalks lead to many of the sites, and visitors are advised to stay on the trail, because parts of this region where the Earth's molten interior escapes to the surface have been known to collapse.

The best time of year to visit is July to October, but make sure to check for road conditions.

▾
The view of Machete Ridge on the Balconies Trail.

STORY BY **DONNA B. ULRICH**
PHOTOS BY **LARRY ULRICH**

PINNACLES

DELIGHTFUL ARRAYS OF PLANTS AND ANIMALS THRIVE AMONG TOWERING ROCK FORMATIONS AND WINDING CAVE TRAILS.

HUGE MONOLITHS AND SHEER CANYONS bear silent witness to Pinnacles National Park's dramatic ancestry as an ancient volcanic field. The San Andreas Fault lies east of the park in central California, and millions of years of faulting, tectonic plate movement and erosion have formed quite spectacular rock formations.

Pinnacles, which had been a national monument, became America's 59th national park in 2013. Situated east of the fertile Salinas Valley in the Gabilan Mountains, Pinnacles is far removed from California's much more famous destinations but is a boon to hikers and rock climbers looking to get away from the crowds.

In 1891 homesteader Schuyler Hain arrived here from Michigan. Over the next 20 years he became known as the "Father of Pinnacles" by leading tours through Bear Valley and writing articles urging preservation of the area. Set aside as a national monument in 1908, Pinnacles' roads and trails were greatly improved by the Civilian Conservation Corps in the mid-1930s.

In spring, when we took our first trip to Pinnacles in eight years, Larry and I were reminded that the area makes us think of Easter. Not only do wildflowers bloom that time of year, but the lichen-covered rocks are a soft pastel color, like Easter eggs nestled in a bed of grass. Blossoms of shooting stars, paintbrush and Johnny-jump-ups paint the green meadows in the exuberant hues of spring.

We hoped to see a California condor, a rare bird re-established at Pinnacles in 2003. With a wingspan reaching 9 feet and beyond, a condor can live for more than 50 years.

Our first stop was the Visitor Center, where we met Sierra Willoughby, an interpretive park ranger. He'd studied geology, so we were not surprised to hear his favorite feature of the park: "Definitely the rocks. There are

Johnny-jump-ups and padre's shooting stars carpet a hillside.

FUN FACTS

In 2003 the park was designated as a national release site for the California Condor Recovery Program. Lucky hikers may spot one of these rare birds.

There are more than 30 miles of tended trails against a backdrop of the endlessly changing hues and textures of eroded volcanic rock.

WORDS TO THE WISE

So-called "wilderness treks" here are for experienced hikers and cave trails are for the would-be spelunkers (don't forget a flashlight). Scaling the Pinnacles' sheer pink cliffs demands experience and special equipment.

Several trailheads are accessible from Bear Gulch Visitor Center. The Moses Spring Self-Guiding Trail climaxes with a visit to the Bear Gulch Reservoir. Hikers who want even more of a challenge can take High Peaks Trail, a 2-mile ramble along the higher reaches.

The park is open year-round and admission is charged.

boulders the size of office buildings, and narrow canyons not unlike those found in Desert Southwest parks like Zion and Bryce. I also appreciate that the park's ecosystem is incredibly intact—the plants and animals have been protected here since 1908. There are about 450 moth, 400 bee and 14 bat species."

As the light faded at our campsite that evening, we watched a cottontail rabbit savor sweet young grass in the nearby meadow. Acorn woodpeckers tapped in the elegant old oaks, the rufous-sided towhee offered its simple tweet and crows cawed to let everybody know who was boss.

At dusk we saw turkey vultures land in a gray pine about 50 feet away. They circled overhead and came to roost one at a time until the tree held at least 50 birds.

We packed for a long day of hiking the next morning. Since the wildflowers were scarce this time, we took Sierra's advice and climbed up the Bear Gulch Cave Trail, entering the caves along the way. The talus caves, formed from narrow canyons crowned with fallen boulders, are famous for their stair-step, zigzag complexity. It's a stoop-and-slide-on-your-behind kind of hike. Bear Gulch Cave is closed from mid-May to mid-July to protect the bat colony as the parents raise their young.

Along the trail we heard one of my favorite birdsongs. The descending melodic trill of the canyon wren never fails to bring my soul into harmony with the boulders and canyons.

On the hike back I saw a big bird soaring in the distance and focused my binoculars—and hopes—on it. I called out to Larry, but he was taking a picture and was not to be distracted. When I saw the white shoulders and then the telltale identification tag on one wing, I knew it was a condor.

We saw only a few bees and didn't see the bats, but the boulders and birds were more than enough to fill our days with beautiful memories. ■

▼
A popular hiking trail leads to Bear Gulch Reservoir.

▼
Boy Scout Tree Trail is in Jedediah Smith Redwoods State Park, part of Redwood National and State Parks.

STORY BY
GORDON AND CATHY ILLG

REDWOOD

TRAVEL BACK THROUGH TIME ALONG THE CALIFORNIA COAST IN THE SHADE OF GIANTS.

LARGE REDWOOD GROVES ARE DEEP, green sanctuaries, where the light is often muted through fog and foliage. They are quiet spaces where normal voices seem harsh and out of place.

But they are also welcoming. These groves are refuges for the human spirit, places of rejuvenation for when the complexity and fast pace of modern living become too much for us.

A 35-mile stretch of U.S. Highway 101 in extreme Northern California is a time machine that transports drivers back millions of years to when ancestors of today's beautiful redwood trees grew all across the Northern Hemisphere.

Today, redwoods are found along the West Coast, starting near the Oregon border and reaching to just south of San Francisco, but the heart of their territory lies along the California coast between Crescent City and Orick. The ideal combination of longitude, climate and elevation helps the trees thrive.

Sixteenth-century Spanish and English mariners were probably the first Europeans to see this part of the world. However, because there were so few good harbors along the coastline, the native Yurok people were relatively sheltered from our young country's westward expansion until 1828, when

POINTS OF INTEREST

NOT TO BE MISSED
At Tall Trees Trailhead (where a free permit is required), a 3-mile loop skirts the 361-foot Howard Libby Tree.

FUN FACT
Signed into being by President Lyndon Johnson and later expanded to 106,000 acres by President Jimmy Carter, Redwood National Park also includes several California state parks, running the Pacific coastline for some 40 miles.

WORDS TO THE WISE
If traveling across the backcountry by bicycle, the Ossagon Trail combines with the Coastal Trail, Davison Road, Streelow Creek, Davison Trail and Newton B. Drury Scenic Parkway in a 19-mile loop.

SIDE TRIP
To see more redwoods, visit Avenue of the Giants. South of Eureka, a 31-mile stretch of old Highway 101 winds through Humboldt Redwoods State Park and the largest old-growth redwood forest in the world.

A curious elk stops to smell the lupines.

Jedediah Smith pioneered an overland route to the redwood forests.

Gold miners also came to explore but found relatively little of the precious metal. The riches of this region are its trees, and by the late 1800s, the timber and lumber industry was king along the Northern California coast.

As entire groves of these giant trees disappeared, concerned citizens began efforts in the 1910s to preserve this scenery for future generations.

The Save the Redwoods League was set up in 1918 as a nonprofit organization committed to acquiring redwood plots for preservation. With private donations and matching state funds, the league purchased more than 100,000 acres of redwood forest from 1920 through 1960.

The California Department of Parks and Recreation created a network of state parks utilizing these lands during the 1920s.

Redwood National Park was established in 1968, and in 1980, the United Nations designated the Redwood national and state parks as a World Heritage Site and Biosphere Reserve.

U.S. Highway 101 runs through this reserve, past the national park and through the Del Norte Coast, Prairie Creek and Jedediah Smith Redwoods state parks, which contain most of the remaining giant redwood trees in the world.

While the entire drive is scenic, there are a couple of side trips that should not be missed. A few miles north of Orick, a short detour takes you to the Lady Bird Johnson Grove, which was dedicated to her in 1969 for her conservation efforts. The 1-mile trail winds through groves of mature redwoods looming out of the fog.

Another great detour is Davison Road, a narrow dirt passage not recommended for trailers or large RVs. What makes the road special is that it leads past Gold Bluffs Beach, where elk can often be seen, and ends at the Fern Canyon Trailhead.

This half-mile trail leads visitors along the bottom of a tight canyon whose 30-foot walls are covered with ferns. It's the sort of place where one would expect to see fairies and wood nymphs living.

One stop that's right on U.S. 101 is not particularly special for most of the year. But when the rhododendrons are blooming in late May and early June, there is no better hike than the Damnation Creek Trail, about halfway between Klamath and Crescent City. Here, the large pink blossoms vie with the trees for your attention, and you don't have to walk far before your senses are overwhelmed.

The oldest redwood trees in the parks sprouted 2,000 years ago, and the largest trees are about 10 feet longer than a football field and more than 65 feet taller than the Statue of Liberty. Humans understandably feel small in their presence.

Redwood groves are truly nature's cathedrals, where we can marvel at and give thanks for the old things, the giant things and the green things that remain. ■

Looking up in Stout Grove at Jedediah Smith Redwoods State Park.

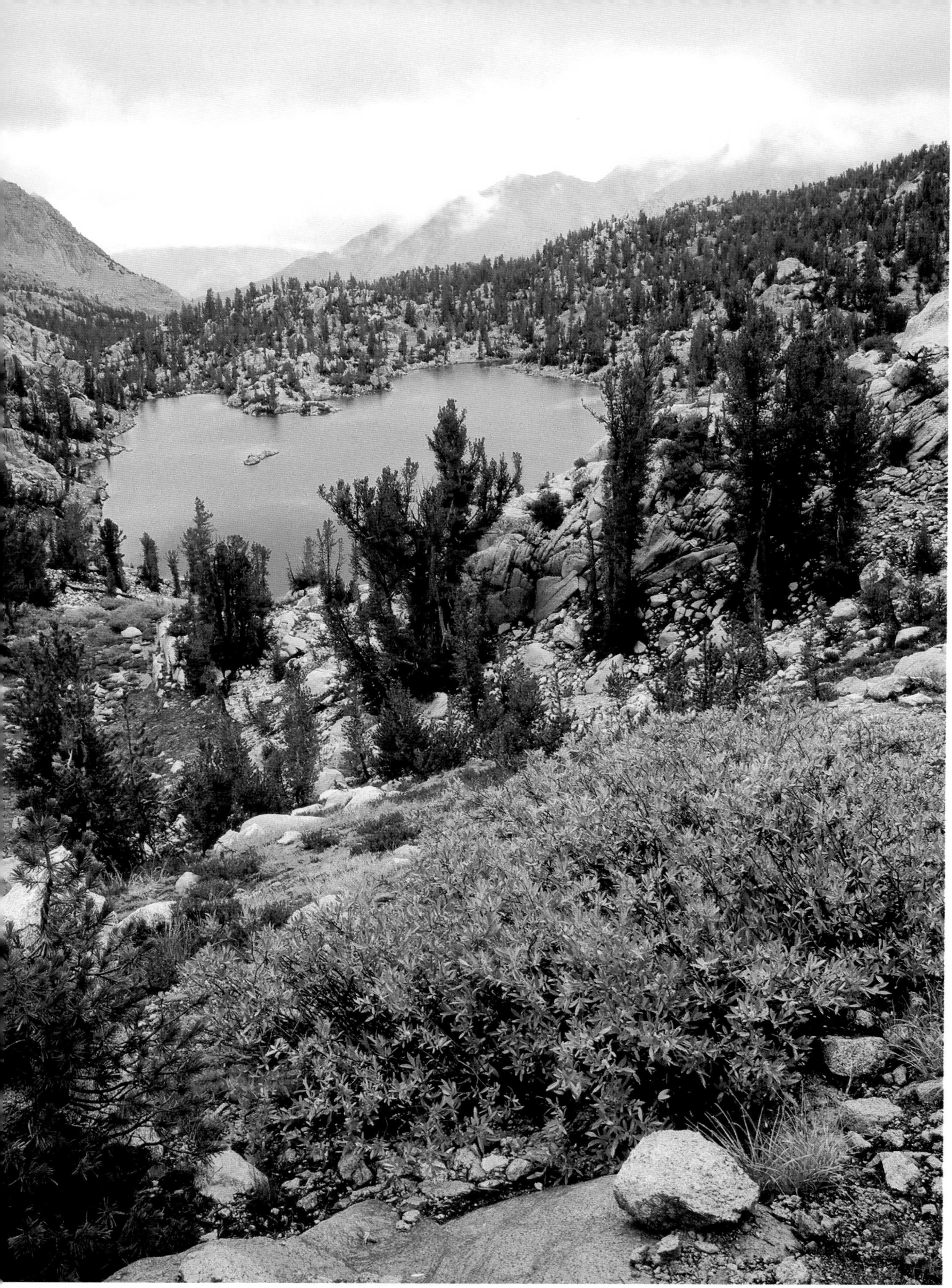

▼
Clearing storm over Sixty Lakes Basin in Kings Canyon.

STORY AND PHOTOS BY
LONDIE GARCIA PADELSKY

SEQUOIA & KINGS CANYON

THE WORLD'S LARGEST TREES RISE ABOVE PRISTINE WILDERNESS IN THE HEART OF CALIFORNIA'S SIERRA NEVADA.

PIONEER NATURALIST JOHN MUIR called California's Sierra Nevada the Range of Light, and you'll still find 1,350 square miles of that dazzling wilderness in Sequoia & Kings Canyon National Parks. You'll also find much smaller crowds than at Yosemite to the north—partly because 90 percent of the park is accessible only on foot or horseback.

Through the years I've spent days, weeks and even months at a time riding and hiking those trails, trying to capture the Sierra Nevada's magic with my camera. But you can also enjoy spectacular scenery from well-tended walking paths or your car. I especially recommend going in April or May, when temperatures are cooler, grasses are greener and the wildflowers are blooming.

Sequoia National Park dates back to 1890, making it the nation's second-oldest national park. General Grant National Park, only a month younger than Sequoia, merged with Kings Canyon when it was named a national park in 1940, and Sequoia and Kings Canyon merged in 1946.

It's almost a full day's drive from my home to the Ash Mountain entrance on the park's southwest corner, and I always look forward to staying in the artists' colony of Three Rivers. The Kaweah River flows through the backyards of the town's stores and restaurants, which means coffee on the deck with a river view.

Heading into the park from the Ash Mountain entrance, Generals Highway climbs more than 5,000 feet on narrow

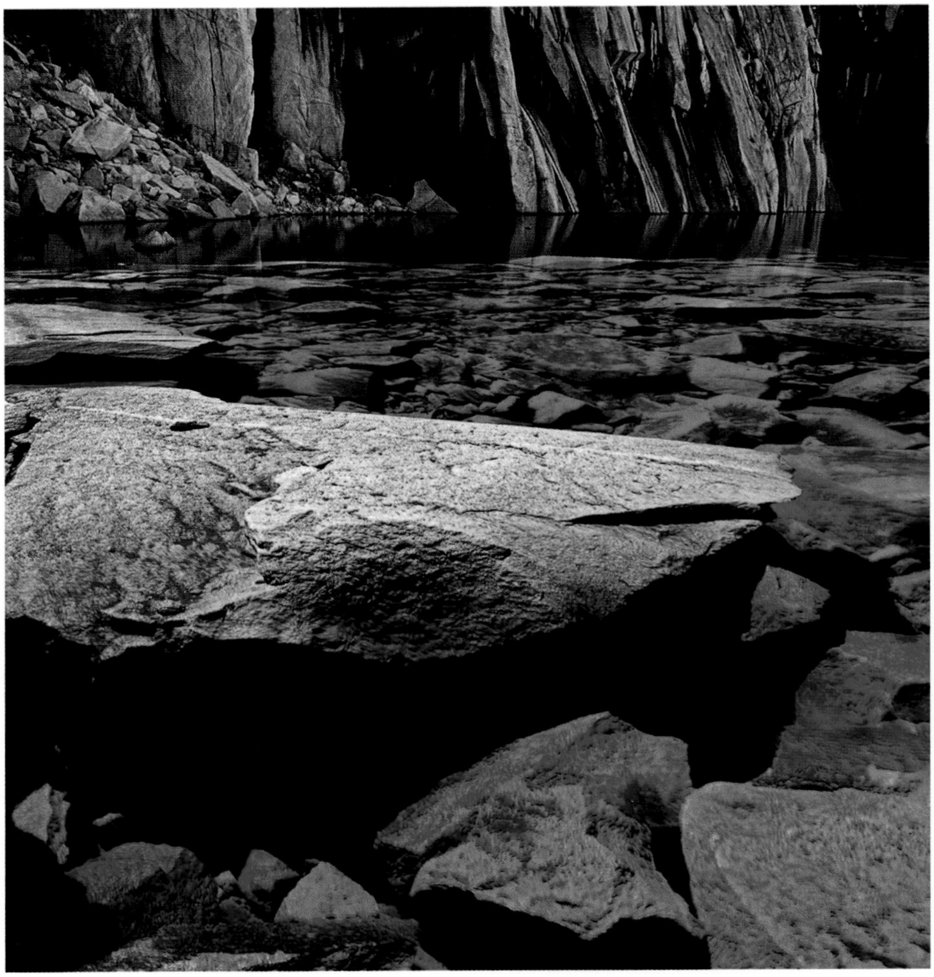

The waters run eerily clear in the remote High Sierra.

POINTS OF INTEREST

NOT TO BE MISSED
Go caving! The park offers a variety of tours through the ornate marble passages of Crystal Cave from May through November. Buy tickets online at least two days in advance on the Sequuoia Parks Conservancy website or at the Foothills or Lodgepole visitor centers.

WORDS TO THE WISE
Be aware that with an elevation range from 1,370 feet to 14,494 feet, weather can vary a lot by season, so dress in layers.

NEARBY ATTRACTIONS
Sequoia National Forest; Sierra National Forest

switchbacks to the edge of the Giant Forest, where four towering sequoias called the Four Guardsmen straddle the highway.

Giant Forest is home to more than 8,000 of these towering trees—half of all the sequoias on the planet. The largest of them, the General Sherman Tree, is 275 feet tall, 100 feet around at the base and an estimated 2,100 years old. Its 52,500 cubic feet of wood make it the largest living thing on Earth. A nearby walking path leads you past a phenomenal display of incredibly massive trees named after the likes of Abraham Lincoln, George Washington, Chief Sequoyah and Benjamin Franklin. I especially like to wander among them on spring weekdays, when there's almost no one on the path.

A short drive away, Moro Rock's granite dome soars above the treetops. A quarter-mile climb up a steep staircase rewards you with spectacular views across the snowcapped peaks of the Great Western Divide. The Moro Rock/ Crescent Meadow Road also features a tunnel log you can drive through and the homestead of pioneer cattleman Hale Tharp. I once spent several lovely hours shooting starflowers here—until a black bear meandered by.

From Giant Forest, Generals Highway heads northward to the Kings Canyon/Grant Grove section of the park. Along the way I like to stop at Lodgepole Visitor Center and take the short hike to Tokopah Falls, where the Kaweah River tumbles down a 1,200-foot staircase of granite.

In the park's northern section, you'll find still more idyllic trails through groves of towering sequoias—including the General Grant Tree, a national shrine to those who died in the Civil War.

But if you're looking for off-the-beaten-path beauty, drive 35 miles beyond Grant Grove on the Kings Canyon Scenic Byway to Cedar Grove. Here you'll find deep-cut canyons, meadows, waterfalls and towering glaciated granite mountains. This hidden paradise is a sampling of nature in the making and a tempting promise of what the Sierra Nevada offers after the road ends.

These backcountry trails usually don't open up until late June or July, and even then the snowpack determines how far you can go. From most of the trailheads, it takes at least two days of hiking or riding over rugged terrain to reach what I call the heart of the Sierra. You have to be self-sufficient in these parts; there are no concessions—only nature, and lots of it.

This wild country is a masterpiece sculpted by the last ice age. Polished granite peaks rise over 14,000 feet from a sea of valleys dotted with thousands of crystalline rivers and lakes. It's a place that continually lures you back, a scenic wilderness that refreshes the mind and rejuvenates the soul. ■

The morning sun shines over giant sequoias and cutleaf coneflowers.

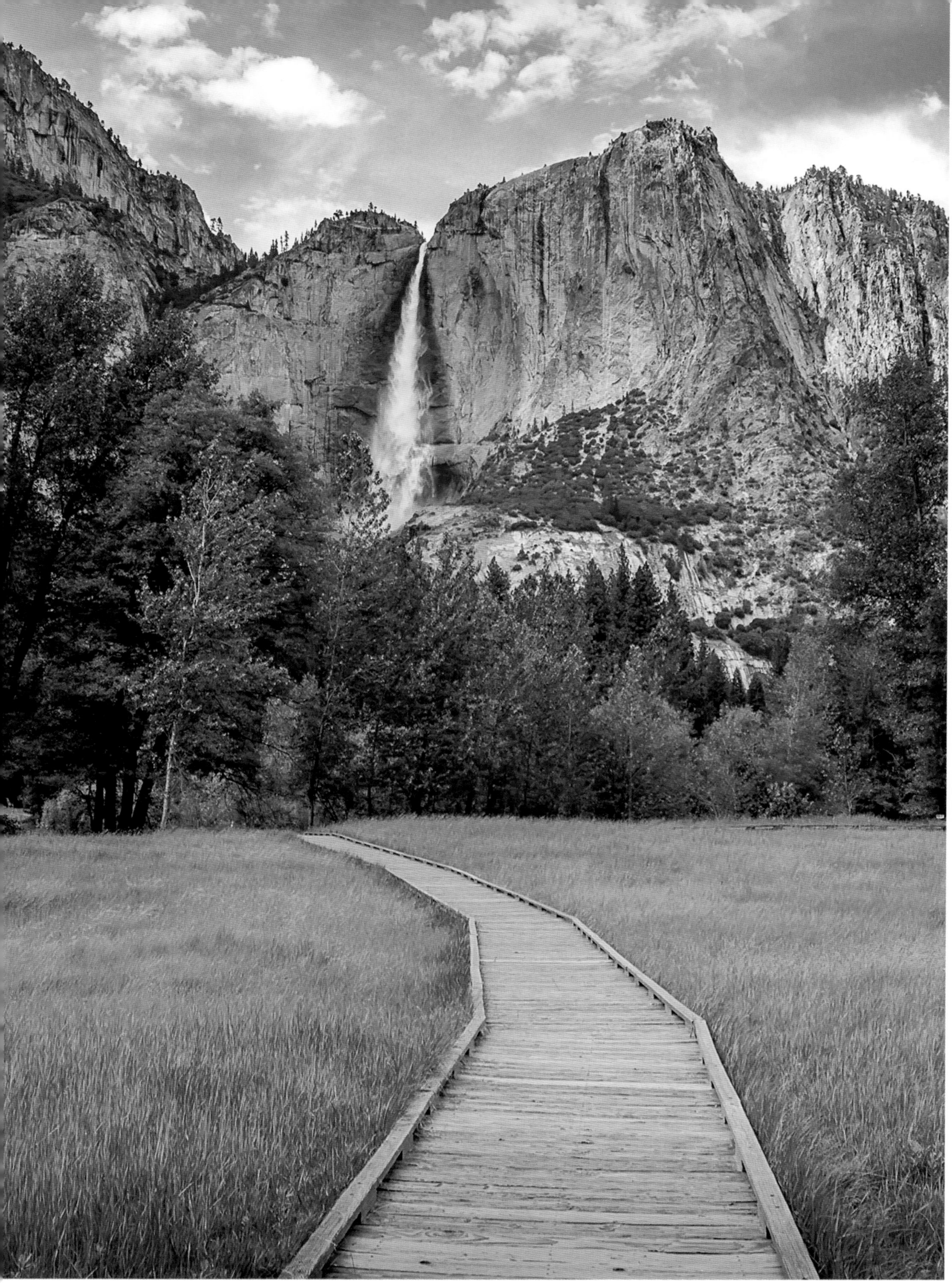

▼
This boardwalk invites visitors to hike through Yosemite Valley in the heart of the park.

STORY AND PHOTOS BY
LONDIE GARCIA PADELSKY

YOSEMITE

JAW-DROPPING MOUNTAIN VISTAS AND CLIFFHANGERS LINE THIS BYWAY THROUGH YOSEMITE NATIONAL PARK.

THOSE OF US LIVING IN the Sierra Nevada know that the heavy snows have begun to melt and spring is about to explode when Tioga Pass Road opens to Yosemite National Park.

At its peak elevation of 9,945 feet, Tioga Pass Road is the highest mountain highway in California. It cuts across Yosemite from the east entrance to Crane Flat in the west. You can drive the road in about two hours, but if you stop for a few excursions it can take all day!

Tioga Pass Road begins on Highway 120 just south of Lee Vining. Right from the start, the road is impressive as you leave the desert sage behind and drive straight toward the high Sierras. When the road weaves to the right, you have an incredible view of Lee Vining Canyon and the two-lane road cutting into a steep mountainside. I don't mind hugging the mountain on the way up—it's the drive down alongside a cliff's edge without any guardrails that puts me on notice.

Come late September, there's a definite nip in the air. That's when the leaves really sparkle in the sunlight. Looking down at Lee Vining Creek from Tioga Pass Road, you view a sea of aspens in vibrant yellow and orange, mixed in with the pine trees. The rich displays of autumn color lure photographers from afar to take pictures of the east side of the Sierra before Tioga Pass closes in November.

At the top of the pass, the road plateaus at Ellery Lake. In a campground nearby, you will find an easy trail to the site of Bennettville, a

POINTS OF INTEREST

REST STOP
Get snacks, gas and music at the Whoa Nellie Deli. The view of Mono Lake is incredible.

FUN FACT
Tioga Pass Road is a fixture in the Sierras. Before John Muir made Yosemite and its environs famous, Native Americans used the road as a footpath. By the 1880s, it became the Great Sierra Wagon Road and connected mines to the railroad.

WORDS TO THE WISE
Depending on weather conditions, Tioga Pass Road usually closes in November and reopens in May. Road updates are available on the National Park Service website. Yosemite is popular in autumn, so plan your visit in advance to beat the crowds.

NEARBY ATTRACTIONS
The Sierra National Forest abuts Yosemite National Park. For a unique way to sample the forest, take the 45-minute ride on the Yosemite Mountain Sugar Pine Railroad, which hauled timber out of the woods beginning in 1899 but now restricts its load to visitors.

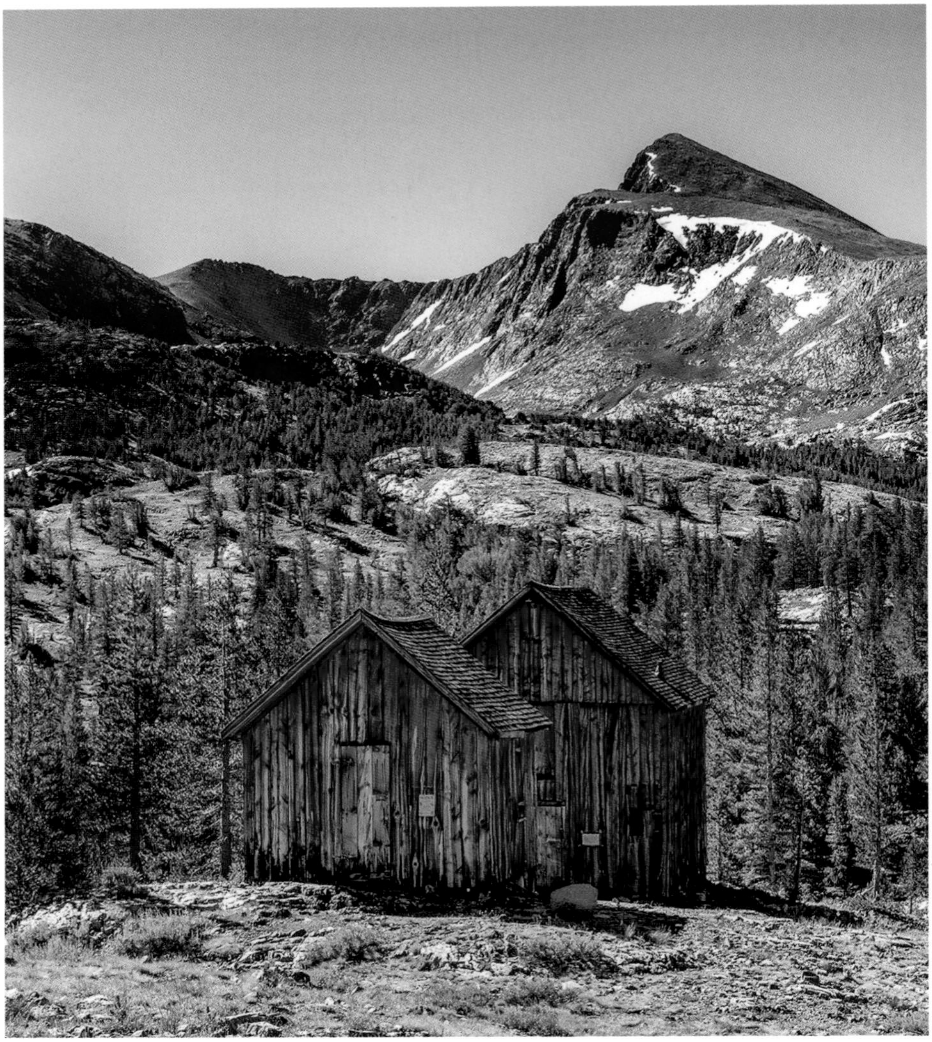

Ruins stand where the mine in Bennettville once boomed.

historic mining town. From there you can hike to some stunning alpine lakes. It's worth the side trip.

Back on the road, continue to the Tioga Pass Entrance Station at the east end of Yosemite. Every time I go through here, I reminisce about legendary Yosemite ranger Ferdinand Castillo, who manned the entrance. For nearly 40 years he had greeted folks with a smile and a joke or some kind of historic Yosemite tidbit. As the story goes, a man once asked Ferdinand what he should do if he had only an hour to visit the park. Ferdinand responded, "See that rock over there? I'd go sit on that rock and cry!"

A sign posted at the entrance station reads "8 miles to Tuolumne Meadows." At 8,600 feet, it is one of the largest subalpine meadows in the Sierra Nevada. The meadows extend far beyond Tioga Pass Road, up the Lyell Fork of the Tuolumne River, where backpackers on the John Muir Trail and Pacific Crest Trail pass through.

My favorite times at Tuolumne Meadows are the early mornings and evenings of spring and summer, when the sunlight brightens and fades across the meadow, and the gray-silver domes and peaks become soft pastels. Few other wanderers are present then, but almost always deer are grazing, coyotes are howling and little pikas are skirmishing about.

Tenaya Lake is a short jaunt from Tuolumne Meadows, and the Tioga Pass Road is just steps from the lakeshore. The Yosemite Indians called it Lake of the Shining Rocks. Here you can fish, canoe, kayak, take an ice-cold dip, or relax on a beach chair and watch the climbers.

Another of my favorite stops is Olmsted Point. From there, a quarter-mile trail leads to an erratic boulder field that seems to have been perfectly placed for travelers who wish to sit and soak in the scenery.

Looking across at the peak known as Clouds Rest and down the valley to Half Dome is amazing; at first glance the distant rounded dome may be unrecognizable. Take your binoculars, as you might be able to see the stream of hikers going up the cables on Half Dome.

From Olmsted Point to Crane Flat, the road demands your attention as it curves with the mountains, although nearly every bend offers a magnificent view. Please be aware that a coyote, deer or black bear could be crossing the road at any time, day or night.

About a mile before Crane Flat at the old Big Oak Flat Road pullout, you can walk on the dirt road through the Tuolumne Grove of giant sequoia trees. One of the many highlights is a 60-foot-high stump with a vehicle tunnel that was cut through in 1878.

Whether you use this amazing mountain road as a mere drive or as a destination, I guarantee that it is one of the most consistently scenic journeys you will ever have the pleasure to experience!

Fallen leaves rest on rocks next to Lee Vining Creek.

STORY AND PHOTOS BY
LAURENCE PARENT

BLACK CANYON OF THE GUNNISON

LEAVE THE LOGJAMS OF TRAVELERS BEHIND AND EXPLORE ONE OF THE MOST DRAMATIC PLACES IN AMERICA.

THE FAINT ROAR OF WHITEWATER drifts up from the abyss at my feet as I cautiously lean over the railing and peer down at the Gunnison River 2,000 feet below. Just a single family shares the overlook with me on this summer afternoon, and I admit the extra elbow room helps make Colorado's Black Canyon of the Gunnison National Park one of my favorite places.

With its sheer, dark gneiss and schist walls shrouded in shadow even in brightest daylight, it's clear where Black Canyon gets its name. I continue along the South Rim Road, stopping at the many overlooks along the way. Each provides an inspiring, vertigo-inducing view of the canyon. At the Painted Wall View, newer molten rock has squeezed through cracks, coloring the massive cliff with pinkish streaks.

At Dragon Point I watch the sunset over the plateau and envy a raven as it dives into the depths, reaching the bottom in moments. The next morning I take a less dramatic trip down to the river along the steep, narrow East Portal Road to Crystal Dam and Reservoir. It's a beautiful drive, but I still yearn to stand beside the river as it rages through the deepest part of the gorge.

So I drive around to the nearly deserted North Rim. And after making sure to check in with a park ranger, I begin my descent—part hike, part scramble—down a narrow ravine. There's no trail, and the route drops 2,000 feet in less than a mile. At the bottom, canyon walls block all but a sliver of the sky and trap the deafening roar of the river as it crashes through rapids and over giant boulders.

I find myself wishing I were that raven, able to fly back to the top of these towering cliffs, but I'm going to have to climb. It's still worth it. That evening, as I once again enjoy the sunset over the canyon, I wonder why more people haven't discovered one of the most striking places in America. ■

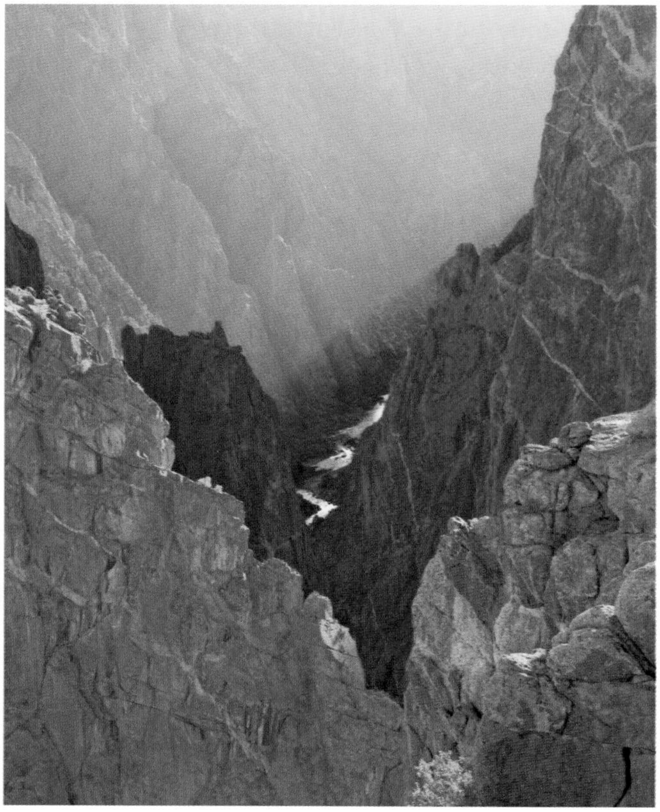

Top: A wind-sculpted juniper hangs on for dear life near Dragon Point. Bottom: Painted Wall plummets 2,250 sheer feet.

NOT TO BE MISSED

The 7-mile South Rim Drive provides spectacular views at its 12 overlooks. Try to allow for 2-3 hours, but if you have limited time, make your stops at Gunnison Point, Chasm View, Painted Wall and Sunset View.

Six more overlooks await on North Rim Road. The canyon walls here are almost vertical. To see all the sights on this side at your leisure, allow 2-3 hours.

FUN FACT

The Gunnison River has a Gold Medal Water & Wild Trout Water designation, which means angling for large trout here is a real treat. Make sure to check out Colorado Parks and Wildlife Fishing Regulations online.

WORDS TO THE WISE

Be aware that many trails have steep drop-offs. Also, bears are in the area, so keep snacks within arm's reach at all times.

STORY BY **SUSAN QUAST**
PHOTO BY **TIM FITZHARRIS**

GREAT SAND DUNES

CLIMB TO WHERE THE SAND MEETS THE SKY FOR AN UNFORGETTABLE TIME IN PARADISE.

THERE'S AN INCREDIBLE SPOT hidden in the mountains of Colorado. It's a place of adventure where kids of all ages can play in Mother Nature's sandbox.

Great Sand Dunes National Park & Preserve, in south-central Colorado, is home to some of the tallest sand dunes in North America. The Sangre de Cristo Mountains provide a dramatic backdrop for the dunes, which are the centerpiece of a diverse landscape of grasslands, wetlands, conifer and aspen forests.

The tallest dune, the Star Dune, is a mere 750 feet high. What a sand pile! It's about a 2.5-mile hike around the entire dune field, and there's no specific trail to follow. Sandboarding and sledding down the dunes are favorite pastimes in the park.

So, how were the dunes made? Most of the sand came from the San Juan Mountains, about 65 miles to the west. Larger grains and pebbles came from the Sangre de Cristos. Sand and sediment from both ranges washed into a huge lake that once covered the valley floor, and as the lake disappeared, winds from the southwest moved the sand into piles. Then winds coming through the mountain passes from the northeast kept piling the dunes back onto themselves, forming the tallest dunes in North America.

After you've hiked, stop and splash in Medano Creek. Depending on the time of year, the creek is just a 6- to 7-foot-wide stretch of damp sand. It begins in the snowfields of the Sangre de Cristos and then cascades down past meadows and into a wide, shallow field. The creek is famous for its surge flow, which creates waves of water on the sand. The creek recedes in July and August, but when its cool waters flow, the sight is just unforgettable.

Regardless of the season, the park offers much to see and do, including camping, hiking and watching for wildlife. With 200 bird species here, birding is another popular activity.

On any clear night, the sky is so dark you can see the Milky Way. Dry air, lack of light pollution and high elevation make the park an ideal spot for stargazing. And if looking up at the heavens is your passion, plan your visit around major astronomical events.

This park isn't as well-known as the Rockies or the scenic train to Durango, but the great dunes are a hidden gem. ■

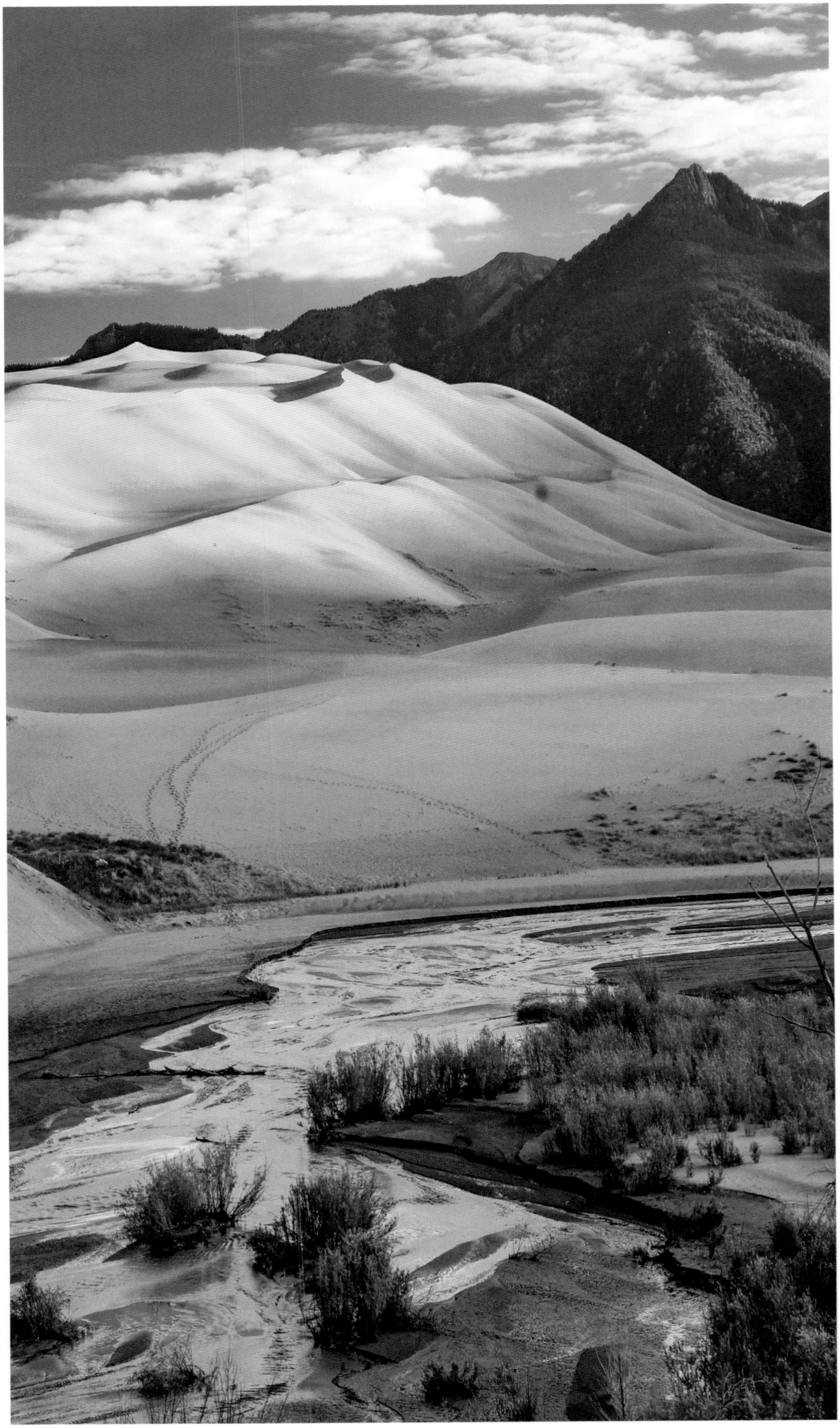

This creek's name, Medano, is Spanish for "sand dune."

NOT TO BE MISSED

Experience the park at night. It is certified as an International Dark Sky Park by the International Dark Sky Association. You can explore dunes, stargaze and listen to the sounds of nocturnal wildlife on your own or led by a ranger.

This unusual park appeals to sand skiers as well as hikers, backpackers, and campers who stay in a campground in an area of junipers and pines at the dunes' edge.

FUN FACTS

Not only are these ever-changing dunes ranked as the tallest in North America, but the dune field stretches over 30 square miles of high mountain-valley floor. The difference between the high and low points in the park (13,604 feet and 7,520 feet) is a whopping 6,084 feet.

WORDS TO THE WISE

The best weather is generally spring and fall. In summer, even though the air temperature is moderate, the sand can get uncomfortably hot.

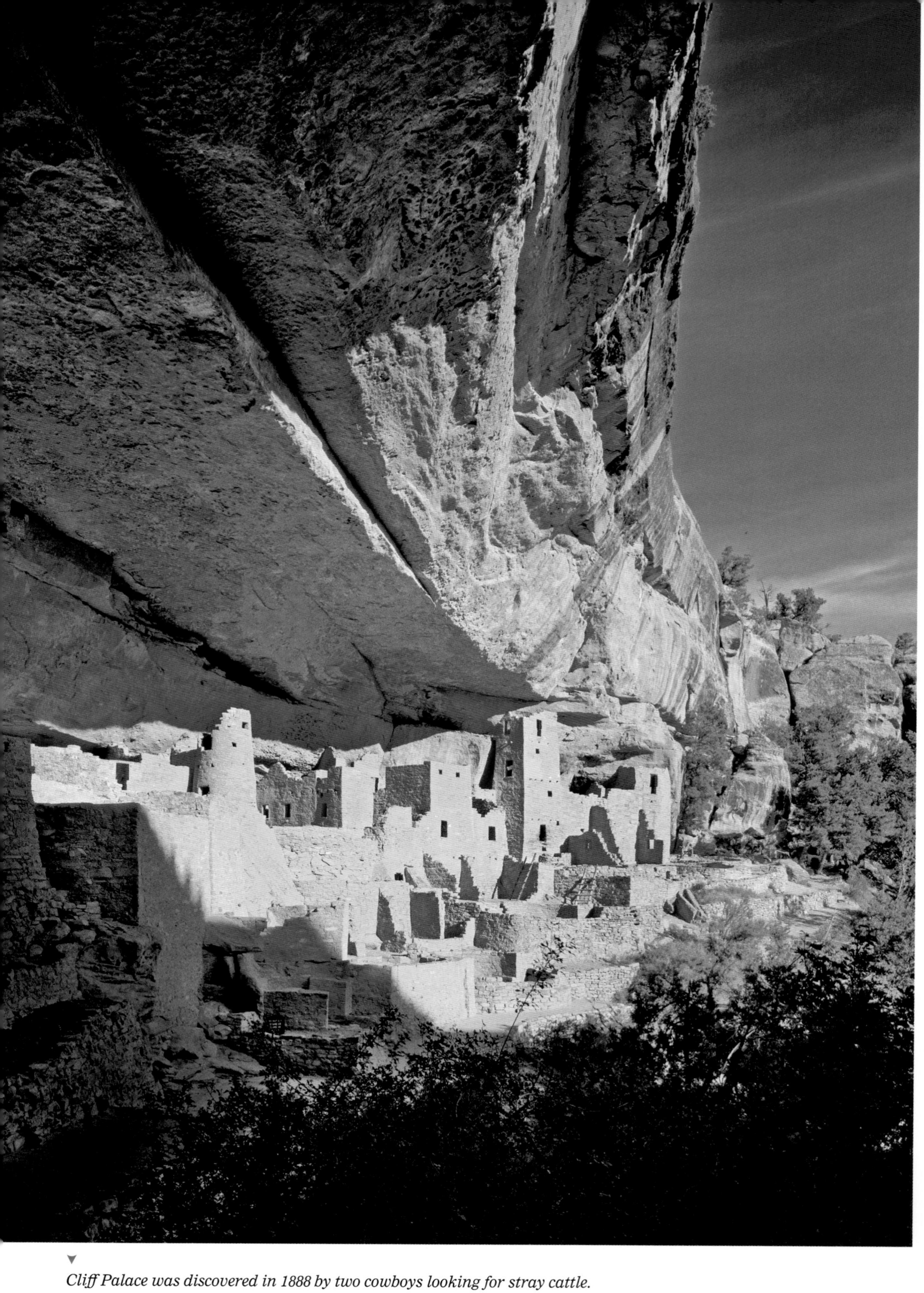

▼
Cliff Palace was discovered in 1888 by two cowboys looking for stray cattle.

Colorado

STORY AND PHOTOS BY
CHRISTOPHER MARONA

MESA VERDE

BREATHTAKING VIEWS STRETCH FOR MILES, BUT A CLOSER LOOK REVEALS ANASAZI DWELLINGS.

STOPPING AT THE ENTRANCE STATION, I rolled down my window. A ranger leaned out and greeted me with a map and brochure. “Enjoy your visit,” he said. Then, almost as an afterthought, he added, “Long House is open today.”

Tucked in the southwest corner of Colorado, Mesa Verde National Park is 10 miles from New Mexico. The name is Spanish for “green table,” and at 8,572 feet above sea level, Park Point is the highest spot of this very tall green table. It affords views stretching across the southwestern landscape to impossible distances.

Immediately to the west, Sleeping Ute Mountain, sacred to local tribes, looks like a napping chieftain with a fanned-out headdress and crossed arms. Farther west in Utah, the La Sal Mountains shimmer in the sun. Just a twist to the south stands Shiprock, New Mexico. Eastward, beyond the green patchwork pastures of the Mancos Valley, the snow-capped La Plata Mountains gleam like the silver for which they are named.

As beautiful as the vistas are, the real treasures of Mesa Verde are those engineered by ancestral Puebloans. These settlers built, occupied and left complex structures more than 300 years before the Pilgrims set foot on Plymouth Rock.

Sometimes called Anasazi, these people inhabited the region 1,400 to 700 years ago. Early structures, called pit houses, were dug into the earth and topped with wooden roofs. As their skills grew, the Anasazi built ceremonial kivas, interconnected rooms with windows and observation towers. In their last era, they created multistory cities perched on the sides of cliffs. Though some dwellings have only three or four rooms, Cliff Palace and Long House both contain more than 100 rooms.

In 1906, President Theodore Roosevelt designated the area a national park, and today UNESCO recognizes it as a World Heritage Site. The National Park Service has restored 35 to 40 structures, but officials estimate there may be 4,500 within park boundaries.

Long House is open today. I could just make the last tour, so I grabbed

POINTS OF INTEREST

NOT TO BE MISSED
At the Chapin Mesa Museum, lifelike dioramas and various exhibits on basket weaving, pottery, masonry and other skills trace the evolution of Puebloan culture from its beginnings in settlements along the Colorado River to its demise nearly eight centuries later.

FUN FACTS
The dwellings were discovered in 1888 when two ranchers, Richard Wetherill and Charlie Mason, set off in a snowstorm in search of stray cattle. Instead they found the preserved Cliff Palace, which was once home to more than 200 ancient Puebloans. The next day, they found Spruce Tree House, naming it for the tree that grew beside the ruin, and Square Tower House, the tallest structure in the park.

The dwellings wisely face south-southwest to keep hot summer rays out but welcome low winter sun.

WORDS TO THE WISE
The park is open year-round, but many sites are closed in winter months.

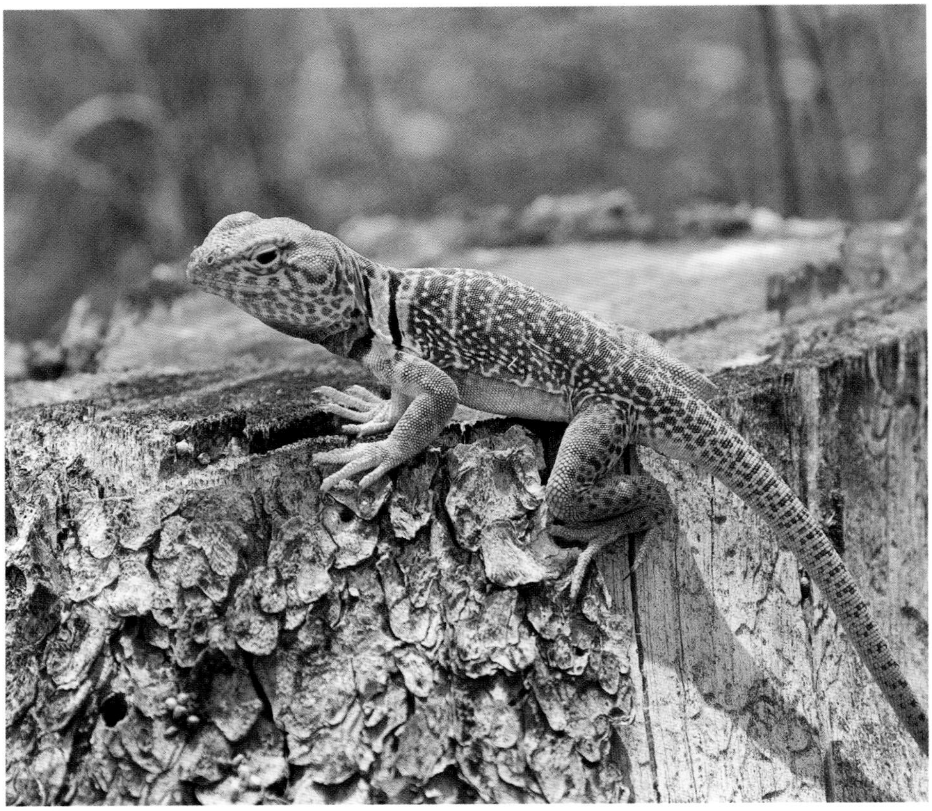

A yellow-headed collared lizard welcomes the rising sun.

my camera bag, tripod and water and boarded the tram. The trail descends 130 feet by switchbacks, stone steps and two 15-foot ladders. Only when you turn the last corner can you see Long House. In the next moment, you are overwhelmed by a massive, overarching rock ceiling and layers upon layers of ancient stone buildings.

I looked down into a circular subterranean room used for political and religious ceremonies. With no windows or doors, the only access would have been through a hole in the roof pierced by a ladder. On the floor, precisely in the center, the Anasazi had dug a small hole. This *sipapu*, as it's called, is found in every structure and symbolizes the tribe's physical and spiritual connection to the earth.

Close examination of the masonry work revealed straight walls, square corners and tightly sealed joints. I peered down over a broken wall into a room that would have served as a home. It was tiny. My guide explained, "Smaller rooms needed fewer materials, took less work to build and were easier to heat."

I was packing my gear when the ranger began to herd the group up the trail. In that moment I realized I was kneeling at the fire pit, where as many as 150 people would have gathered 800 years ago.

On the mesa top, the ranger waited to lock the gate. I asked for his opinion about how large an area the ancestral Puebloans had roamed. He replied, "From here to there—we believe there are at least 40,000 unique archaeological sites," and he swept his finger across the horizon.

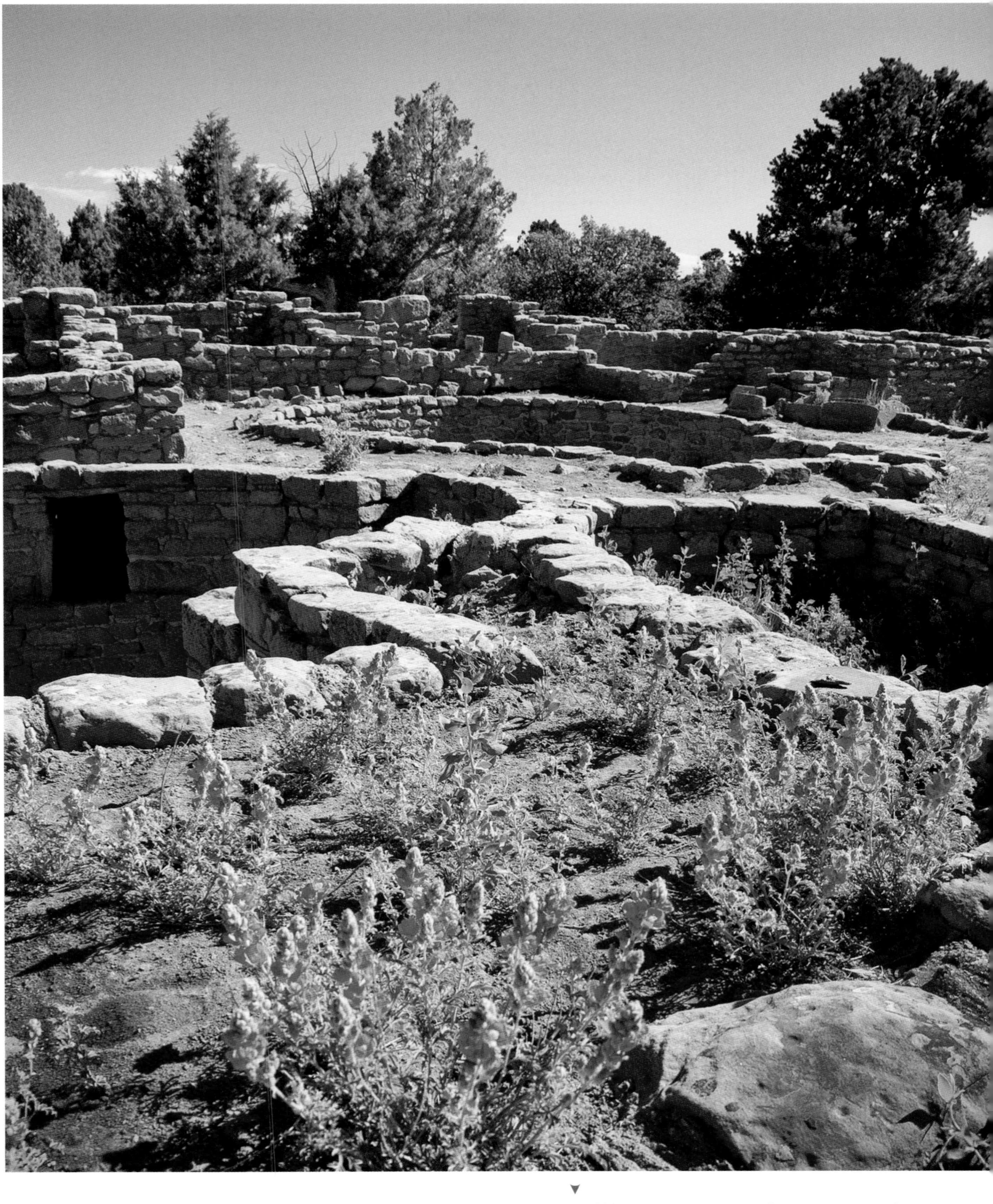

Wildflowers bloom on ancient mesa-top ruins.

▼
The sweeping view of Odessa Lake from the side of Joe Mills Mountain.

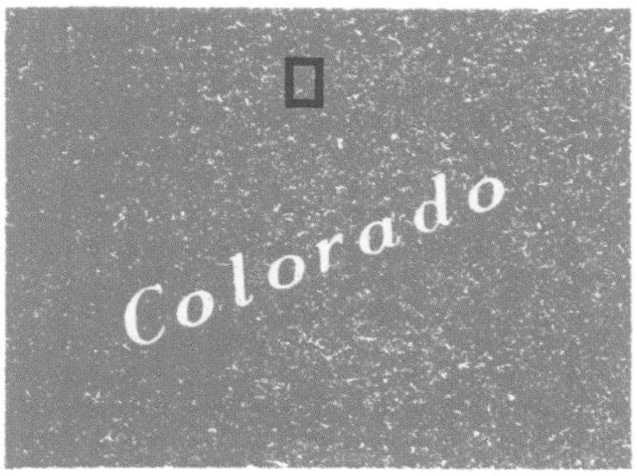

STORY BY
DAN BLACKBURN

ROCKY MOUNTAIN

FEEL ON TOP OF THE WORLD VISITING THIS WELL-KNOWN MUST-SEE NATIONAL PARK IN THE MIDDLE OF NORTH AMERICA.

IN THE ARMY, A BUGLER BLASTS you out of bed at dawn. In Rocky Mountain National Park, you may also be awakened by early-morning bugling, but a large elk with horns on its head provides the music. My wife, Gloria, and I hear an elk and rise from our tent.

On Sept. 4, 1915, 200-300 people assembled in Colorado's Horseshoe Park to celebrate the dedication of a new American treasure. U.S. Rep. Edward Taylor and Gov. George Carlson joined naturalist Enos Mills, who was instrumental in getting the park developed. President Woodrow Wilson had signed the order into law in January of that year, designating another beautiful national park.

The park sprawls across 415 square miles of widely varied terrain, from alpine tundra to pine forests and even wetlands, and encompasses more than 100 peaks rising above 10,000 feet as it spans the famed Continental Divide. The tallest is Longs Peak, a towering 14,259 feet high, visible throughout much of the park and reflected in several crystalline lakes. Dream Lake is reportedly the most photographed, but there are plenty of breathtaking alternatives to explore.

Ninety-five percent of Rocky Mountain National Park is protected as wilderness. This makes it a hiker's paradise with scores of trails, many of them used by American Indian hunters centuries ago. On these largely unchanged paths, it is easy to become immersed in the forest and revel in the tumbling sounds of water from rushing mountain falls and streams.

Snow blankets much of the park in winter, but the arrival of spring usually sees the snow retreat back to higher

In the backcountry this bull moose quietly grazes in wetlands.

POINTS OF INTEREST

NOT TO BE MISSED

Intrepid visitors may choose to stay at the famous Stanley Hotel in Estes Park, which served as the inspiration for Stephen King's *The Shining.*

Hikers who explore the Colorado River District trails on the western side of the Continental Divide are rewarded with views of Grand Lake as they climb the Devil's Staircase.

FUN FACT

Ninety-five percent of the park's 265,873 acres is protected as wilderness, with more than 350 miles of amazing hiking trails to explore.

WORDS TO THE WISE

Beware of lightning along Trail Ridge Road. It is usually open May to October, weather permitting; other roads are open year-round.

elevations. Trail Ridge Road closes in mid- to late October and, thanks to plowing, can reopen in late May.

This famous 48-mile-long scenic drive, the highest continuous paved highway in the U.S., climbs above 12,000 feet, offering visitors spectacular vistas of the Rocky Mountains in all directions.

Summer means blooming wildflowers and herds of people, as it's time for family vacations, and the park's easy access from Denver beckons schoolchildren and their parents. The park is definitely popular and one of the most-visited national parks.

Gloria and I are enthusiasts of the national parks, steadily working on our goal of visiting as many as we can from the Rocky Mountains to the West Coast. We're also dedicated tent campers. As we researched our trip, we heard the five campgrounds here were very good, and I'm happy to report this is true.

We pitched our tent in Moraine Park campground, nestled in a ponderosa pine forest above meadows. We visited in the fall, when the crowds are much smaller. The Big Thompson River runs through Moraine Park, attracting a variety of wildlife. On several days, we had mule deer grazing within a stone's throw of our campsite.

This campground is a good home base for exploring some highlights of the park. Bear Lake Road, another scenic drive, begins here and goes 9.3 miles into the core of the Glacier Gorge area to Bear Lake, a sparkling jewel surrounded by dramatic mountain peaks at the foot of the Continental Divide.

For hikers, the Fern Lake and Cub Lake trailheads, both near the campground, are pathways to gorgeous waterfalls, lakes and mountains. Go in autumn and revel in the brilliant golden glow as the leaves on the aspens turn.

Even though there's much to explore, the bugling of the elk kept calling us back to the meadows. The male elk use this distinctive sound to summon the females to join their respective herds. Occasionally a younger male will challenge an older bull, and the clash of their massive horns echoes through the forests and across the meadows. The winner gets the harem.

Sometimes a wandering moose strays into the elk meadows, but none of the elk is foolish enough to challenge those big bulls. A visiting moose will survey the scene much like a tourist before moving on.

Painters capturing nature's beauty with oils or watercolors often spread throughout the park, and we spend some time looking over their shoulders while they graciously share their work and thoughts with us.

After a week, we concluded that the park is simply too large and diverse to experience in just one visit. Its size and variety border on daunting. Rocky Mountain National Park simply will have to go back on our list to happily return to again and again. ■

Yellow wildflowers along Trail Ridge Road await the sun. ◄

LEFT: JOHN KUPPA; RIGHT: RONDAKIMBROW/GETTY IMAGES

1.

2.

1. TRAIL OF THE CEDARS
Taken on a trip to Glacier National Park in the summer, this photo shows an inviting trail through giant evergreens. At one point the trail crosses Avalanche Creek as it winds through the forest.
– **ELIZABETH BOULTER**

2. SCHWABACHER LANDING
The sun rose behind me and illuminated the top of Grand Teton Mountain at Grand Teton National Park. Smoke from mountain wildfires contributed to the reddish skies. – **KEN SMITH**

3. MESA ARCH
A brilliant sunrise at Canyonlands National Park in southern Utah. From this spot it feels as if you're standing on nature's balcony and peeking under the canyon's covers. – **JUDITH FULLER**

4. GRAND PRISMATIC SPRING
One of the most color-filled locations in Yellowstone National Park, this is my ultimate favorite spot to see and photograph. It's as unique as a fingerprint and is constantly changing. – **RENEE LUND**

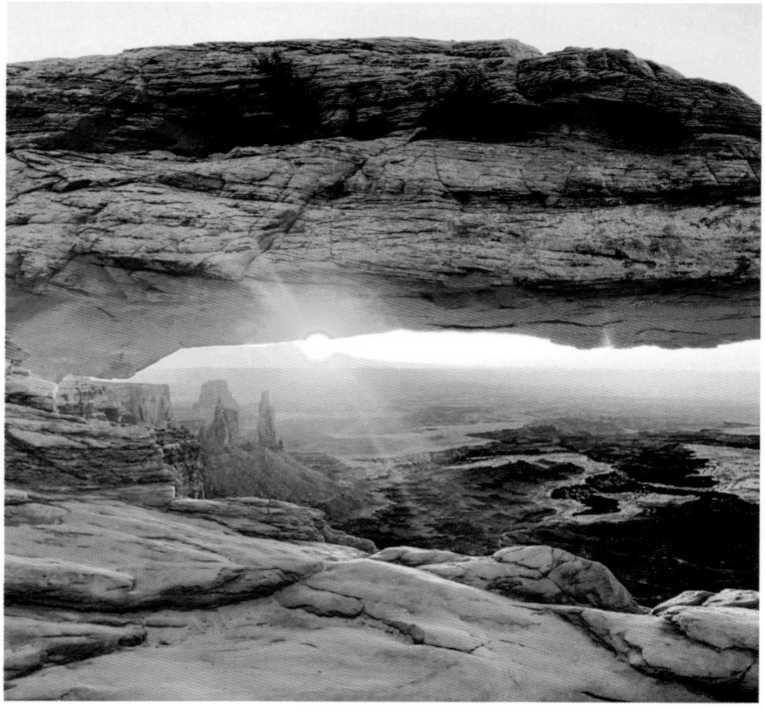
3.

4.

1.

2.

3.

4.

1. BACKPACKING INTO THE DUNES
The wind was fierce during sunset at Great Sand Dunes National Park and the temperature was quickly dropping. –**JON RUFFOLO**

2. RUSHING WATERS
My brother, standing on the log above the Sol Duc Falls in Olympic National Park, illustrates the scale of the scene. When someone well over 6 feet tall is dwarfed by their surroundings, you can imagine the magnitude in person. –**ELISE MORRIS**

3. WATCHMAN
I love this classic close-up of the Watchman at sunset in Zion National Park. I am in awe of the vibrant color and details in the rock formations. I think it would look different every evening. –**THOMAS GUFFY**

4. TUNDRA SWAN
I waded through 3 feet of snow and was rewarded with this swan flapping its wings in Yellowstone National Park. –**BARRY SAMUEL**

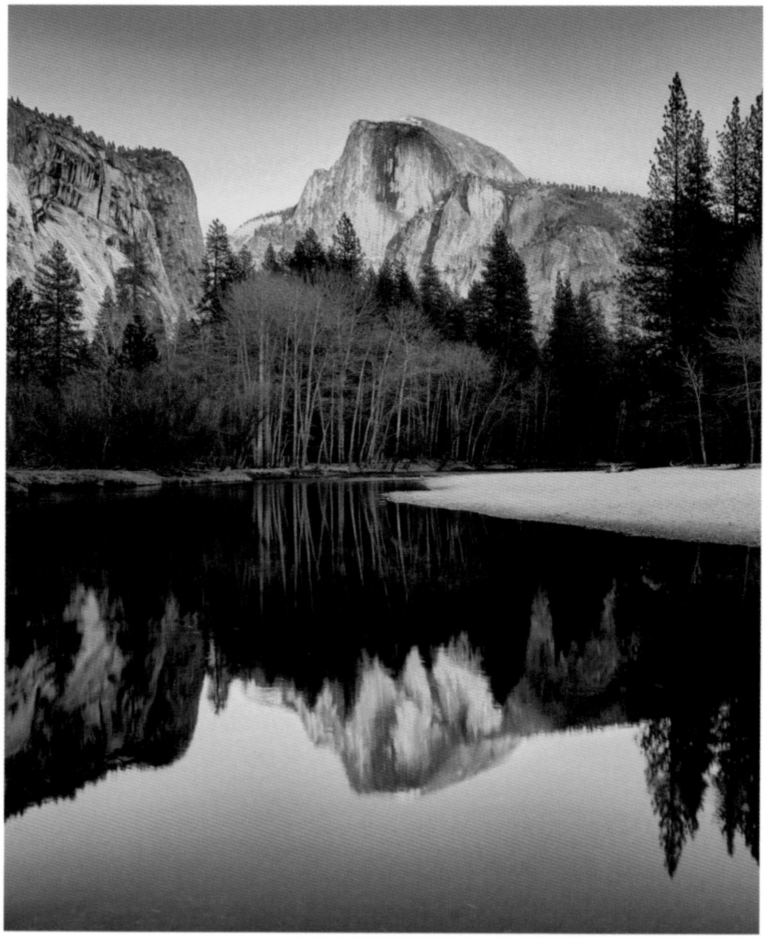

1.

1. HALF DOME
This recognizable rock face is at the eastern end of Yosemite Valley in Yosemite National Park. It was evening when the sun's rays fell on the dome, with the smooth Merced River in the foreground. – **GEORGE WIEDENHOFER**

2. LOGAN PASS
I spent about three hours at this location in Glacier National Park. As I hiked around the trails, I was amazed at the number of bighorn sheep, mountain goats and deer. – **MICHAEL SASS**

3. EARLY RISER
Canyonlands National Park offers the most stunning sunrises and sunsets I have ever seen. The colors are breathtaking. Definitely worth getting into the park early to take in a sunrise. – **BARRY WILLIAMS**

4. HISTORICAL HOMESTEAD
The Moulton family built this barn in Grand Teton National Park. I love to imagine what it must have been like for homesteaders over a century ago, building their homes with views of the Tetons. – **JULIA BLANTON**

5. MAJESTIC TREES
The beauty of Redwood National and State Parks is definitely underrated. Walking among these giant ancient trees was a humbling experience. – **KATARINA BATES**

2.

3.

4.

5.

▼
Life is renewed as a'e ferns grow out of cracks in dried lava in Hawaii Volcanoes National Park.

STORY BY **CATHY ILLG**
PHOTOS BY **GORDON ILLG**

HAWAII VOLCANOES

THE BIG ISLAND OFFERS A FRONT ROW SEAT TO EARTH'S MAGNIFICENT TRANSFORMATION.

OUR SURROUNDINGS WERE PITCH BLACK, but in our headlamps we could see bits and pieces of rough, twisted terrain so sharp that any bare skin that touched it came away wounded

We were stumbling in the dark with our guides, photographers CJ Kale and Nick Selway, to see the expansion of new land formed by lava on Hawaii, the Big Island of the Hawaiian Islands. They own Lava Light Gallery in Kailua-Kona, and likely have more photos of running lava than anyone else in the world.

The cracks we were stepping over glowed orange, and the heat was intense. CJ and Nick led us through the darkness to the island's western edge, where we could go no farther.

Earth is a constantly moving jigsaw puzzle, and nowhere is that more evident than the Big Island. The tectonic Pacific Plate is inching northwest over a weak spot in the Earth's crust that is more or less continuously leaking magma. Over time, enough lava has flowed to create an archipelago, or chain of islands, in the middle of the Pacific Ocean, and the process is still ongoing.

At more than twice the size of all the other Hawaiian islands combined, the Big Island offers something for everyone. And it is home to the must-see Hawaii Volcanoes National Park, founded Aug. 1, 1916.

In contrast to our rugged journey on foot, it's easy to explore the park via car. Kilauea Volcano, which has been erupting pretty much continuously since 1983, should be on every visitor's list. Crater Rim Drive, an 11-mile road, provides access to scenic points and short walking trails. Be sure to stop at the Kilauea Visitor Center before you begin your trip, because road conditions around active volcanoes may change with little notice.

For much of the eruption, lava flowing out of Kilauea has crossed

▼ *An i'iwi feeds on an ohia lehua blossom.*

POINTS OF INTEREST

NOT TO BE MISSED
Kilauea Volcano, inside the park. Take scenic Crater Rim Drive, which encircles the volcano.

Mauna Loa (Long Mountain) is the largest volcano on Earth, covering half the surface of the Big Island. Located inside the park, it last erupted in 1984.

NEARBY ATTRACTIONS
To reach the top of dormant Mauna Kea (White Mountain) you can drive from sea level to 13,796 feet in 2 hours—or hike from the Visitor Information Station at 9,200 feet in about 8 hours.

Akaka Falls, with a dramatic drop of 442 feet, can be reached via a short, paved path. The loop also passes by Kahuna Falls. At nearby Rainbow Falls, the Wailuku River rushes over a rocky archway, and the morning sun creates rainbows in the mist.

national park land toward the sea. But in 2014, a breakout of lava began to flow across private property to the east. If you wish to view the lava, make sure you go with a guide who has permission to access this property.

We watched from a safe distance nearby as the molten rock oozed its way downhill. It popped and it crackled, forming ropes and ribbons of incandescent colors. Where the lava poured into the pounding surf, it hissed, sending up clouds of steam.

The island's twin volcanic peaks of Mauna Loa and Mauna Kea are the tallest mountains on Earth—if you measure them from the ocean floor. Reaching to nearly 14,000 feet above sea level, they give massive testament to the amount of magma that has leaked out of the earth.

We drove high up the mountains to where there was frost on the tropical vegetation. When most people think of Hawaii, they think of white sand, not white snow. But it's true: Mauna Kea and Mauna Loa are often snowcapped in winter. In fact, the name Mauna Kea means White Mountain, and the road to the summit has been closed due to heavy snow.

Because they block the trade winds, these mountains divide the island into one of the world's wettest places on the east side and a desert on the west.

Sun worshippers will flock to the beaches of the Kona and Kohala Coasts on the dry western side of the island. But the rainforests north of Hilo on the east coast are just the ticket for those drawn to verdant landscapes. Maybe it's because we live in the arid American West, but these densely forested slopes feel simply magical.

Some of the largest, most scenic and most easily accessible waterfalls in the state can be found in this area: the 442-foot Akaka Falls and 80-foot Rainbow Falls on the outskirts of Hilo. And if you enjoy colorful blooms and lush jungles, the Hawaii Tropical Botanical Garden is just a 10-minute drive north of Hilo.

While we were bouncing over a rough road on the eastern slopes of Mauna Kea, our guide and fellow photographer, Jack Jeffrey, told us he wanted to show us something special. Jack is a retired wildlife biologist with the Fish & Wildlife Service, and he's directly responsible for returning a large chunk of this forest to its natural state. He was taking us to the Hakalau Forest National Wildlife Refuge.

Hawaii is the most isolated island chain in the world. Species had to travel immense distances to reach these cooling volcanoes, and the surrounding ocean is miles deep. As these bare rocks rose above the waters, they were visited by life that was probably lost at sea: a plant seed here, a bird there. And from these colonists, new native species developed. Hakalau is one of the best places in Hawaii to see the fabulous native birds, and having a guide like Jack, who knows them better than anyone, will help you spot them.

The flamboyant and brilliantly colored honeycreepers owe their existence to some long-ago marooned finches. With names like amakihi, apapane and i'iwi, their beaks come in sizes and shapes that boggle the imagination. Watching an i'iwi probe an ohia lehua blossom for nectar was a much bigger thrill than becoming another sunburned tourist on the beach.

When you do go to the shore, we highly recommend poking your head under the waves to check out Hawaii's native fish; many species are found only here. Our favorite snorkeling spots are all on the sunnier, west side of the island. Kahalu'u Beach has shallow water, no dangerous currents and a bounty of fish and green sea turtles.

All of the Hawaiian Islands are truly gifts from the sea. But only the Big Island offers the opportunity to see how these islands were formed, such as in a place like Hawaii Volcanoes National Park. Marvel at the metamorphosis that has transformed the black, twisted landscapes of molten rock into paradise! ■

▼ *The beauty of Akaka Falls speaks for itself.*

RIGHT: GEORGE H.H. HUEY/ALAMY STOCK PHOTO

▼
A carpet of color contrasts with the snow on Garden Wall in Glacier.

STORY BY **KARIN LEPERI AND CHUCK HANEY**
PHOTOS BY **CHUCK HANEY**

GLACIER

FALL AND SUMMER COLORS REALLY ENHANCE THE TRUE BEAUTY OF THIS SPECIAL PLACE IN MONTANA.

FOR DRAMATIC FALL LANDSCAPES, it's hard to beat Going-to-the-Sun Road over Logan Pass in Glacier National Park. A snakelike highway that seems to melt into the sun, the 50-mile, two-lane road was named after a Blackfoot Indian spirit who came to earth and returned to the sky via the mountain.

Here in the northern Rockies, an explosion of color contrasts starkly against cedar, evergreens and snow-covered jagged peaks. The golds and yellows from aspen and western larch, oranges and reds from ash, and huckleberry crimson provide a blazing palette of nature's glory. Amid air as crisp as Winesap apples, expect to encounter wildlife such as mountain goats, bighorn sheep, elk, moose and even grizzlies along the way as they prepare for the long winter ahead.

September is the best month for viewing aspen, birch, cottonwood and huckleberry. Mid-October is best for western larch. You'll see yellow-gold (aspen, birch, cottonwood, western larch); orange (Rocky Mountain maple); orange-red (mountain ash); crimson (huckleberry); and green (juniper, cypress, ever-greens) as well.

If you are looking for a hiking experience among yellowing larch (also known as tamarack), choose any of the trails from Sperry Trailhead near Lake McDonald Lodge. This is bear country though, so make sure to take safety precautions and dress for variable weather conditions.

For some pedaling, just outside of the park you'll find an easy bike ride along an old railroad bed that became a bike trail. The path follows the old rail route past several highlights in the Flathead Valley, including Whitefish and Flathead lakes. For more info, visit the website of the Rails to Trails of Northwest Montana organization.

▼ *Nature paints a vibrant still life with wildflowers in the park.*

POINTS OF INTEREST

NOT TO BE MISSED

Flowers to look for in summer include:

- beargrass
- glacier lily
- clematis
- purple aster
- western anemone
- lupine
- mountain lady's slipper
- Lewis's monkeyflower
- trillium
- blanket flower

FUN FACT

Glacier National Park is home to thousands of mountain goats, and with good reason. These sure-footed climbers prefer high elevations and can easily ascend steep, rocky slopes that are 60 degrees or more. You will often find them resting on the rocky cliffs, away from predators,or—to make up for the salt they lack in their diet—licking the mineral-rich rock in an area of the park known as Goat Lick.

NEARBY ATTRACTION

Waterton Lakes National Park, contiguous to Glacier, lies north of the U.S.-Canada border. The two together are known as Waterton-Glacier International Peace Park.

To camp, fall is a fantastic time to sleep under the stars in Glacier. The only auto campgrounds open by Nov. 1 are the Apgar and St. Mary campgrounds, both of which have no fees during the winter.

If you really do want to avoid the crowds, fall is likely the best time. You will, however, have to be self-sufficient, as many concessions will closed down for the season.

For another kind of colorful display, Glacier, also known as the Crown of the Continent, bursts with vibrant stands of prairie and alpine wildflowers during its brief summer season. With more than 730 miles of hiking trails that provide access to soaring peaks, mountain meadows, lush tracts of forest and clear, fish-filled lakes, the park offers countless places to view summer blossoms.

By early July, a vast array of prairie wildflowers, including lupines and blanket flowers, appears along roadways in the St. Mary and many Glacier valleys. The blooms move higher in elevation as the summer progresses.

The alpine meadows at Logan Pass are among the most beautiful spots on the planet. The best bet to take in all the glory of the flora is to walk 1.5 miles from the Logan Pass Visitor Center to the Hidden Lake Overlook. Most of the path is on a boardwalk to help protect the fragile environment.

Heading north from the visitor center, the 11.4-mile Highline Trail leads hikers along the west side of the park's resplendent and aptly named Garden Wall.

In late July, yellow glacier lilies emerge as the lingering snowfields begin to melt and recede, and by early August, it is a bloom fest with a variety of colorful wildflowers spread across the meadows. My favorites are the stands of Lewis's monkeyflowers, which add a layer of vibrancy to the red rock outcroppings.

Whenever you decide to go, the majesty of Glacier will draw you in. ■

Aspens at peak color are hard not to notice.

STORY BY **DONNA B. ULRICH**
PHOTOS BY **LARRY ULRICH**

GREAT BASIN

WHEELER PEAK PRESIDES OVER LAKES, VALLEYS, LIMESTONE CAVES AND SOME OF THE OLDEST TREES ON THE PLANET.

GREAT BASIN NATIONAL PARK has everything from snow-covered peaks and alpine lakes to trees as old as the hills. What it doesn't have is a major city nearby, unless you count Baker, Nevada, population around 60. If you like the thought of a park without cars and buses packed into parking lots, take this little side trip off what *Life* magazine once labeled "The Loneliest Road in America," Highway 50.

You'll find the park on the eastern edge of the Basin and Range Province, the region extending east from California's Sierra Nevada to Utah's Wasatch Range, and from southern Oregon to southern Nevada. A distinguishing feature is that all of the region's rivers flow inland, not to the ocean.

At 13,063 feet, Wheeler Peak soars above the desert valleys and dominates the skyline. The 12-mile Wheeler Peak Scenic Drive climbs nearly 3,000 feet from the park boundary to its terminus at 10,000 feet. At the road's end are a campground, trailheads for climbing, high mountain lakes and a bristlecone pine forest. The popular Alpine Loops trail passes by Teresa and Stella lakes, both above 10,000 feet.

Bristlecone pines are among the oldest trees on Earth; some were young when the Egyptian pyramids were under construction. In 1964, one pine tree on Wheeler Peak was determined to be 4,862 years old. Fantastically twisted, gnarled and fastened to the earth with roots like steel, bristlecone pines tell a tale of struggle for survival on barren, rocky, windblown terrain. The wood, worn smooth by the elements, has a sculpted beauty not unlike polished stone.

Down on Wheeler's flank are the Lehman Caves and the impressive Lexington Arch, carved out of limestone by ancient waters. It's thought that the arch was once part of a passage in a cave system.

When the high desert is awash with Indian paintbrush, desert dandelion and prickly pear cactus, all scattered in sagebrush, the park is a happy oasis off the Loneliest Road in America.

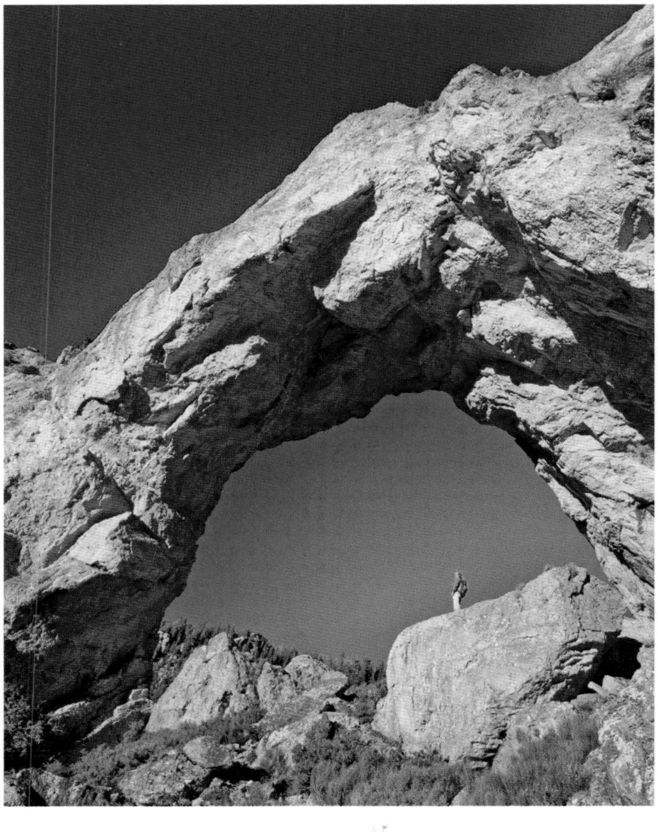

Top: An aspen grove beneath the sheer rock face of Wheeler Peak. Bottom: The rugged landscape is no match for a hardy hiker at Lexington Arch.

POINTS OF INTEREST

NOT TO BE MISSED

Stargaze in this designated International Dark Sky Park where you can see the Milky Way with the naked eye on a summer night. There's an annual Astronomy Festival, star train rides, a full moon hike and solar telescope viewing.

Spend a day fishing in Lehman Creek, or visit Upper Pictograph Cave to see ancient Fremont Indian rock art.

FUN FACTS

Sweeping across 77,000 acres, the park's drastic elevation changes—from desert valley floor to 13,000-foot Wheeler Peak—encompass springs, fossils, subterranean caves, a glacier, and dizzying arrays of plant, animal and bird species.

WORDS TO THE WISE

Visit in summer to early fall.

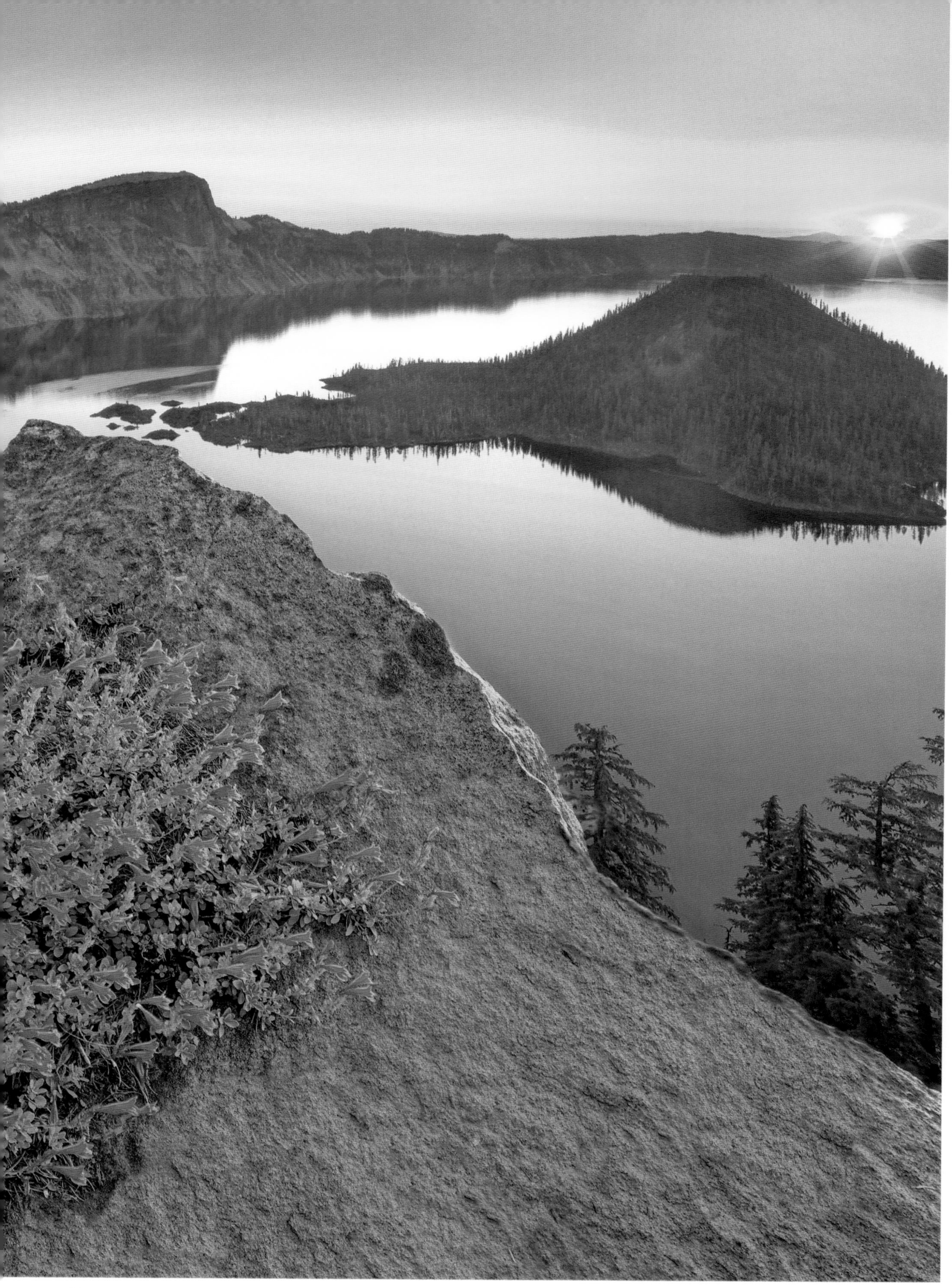

▼
The park has 400 species of plants, including penstemon.

STORY AND PHOTOS BY
DENNIS FRATES

CRATER LAKE

DIVE RIGHT IN TO THE SPLENDOR AND MYSTERY OF THIS NATURAL WONDER IN OREGON.

THE FIRST TIME my then-10-year-old daughter saw Crater Lake National Park, her jaw just dropped. Before her were the deep blue waters of a lake surrounded by jagged peaks—the remains of a mighty mountain known as Mazama.

"You told me this was a beautiful lake, but I had no idea it was this incredible," Nicki said at the time.

That is the Crater Lake effect. This magical and majestic place is the only national park in Oregon and the deepest lake in the United States. Though Crater Lake isn't among the most visited national parks, it should be. It is an awe-inspiring weekend getaway. Included here are things that I love to do at this scenic wonder.

Driving the rim is definitely tops. Crater Lake's rim rises 8,000 feet, allowing snow to remain until early summer. The best time to visit is in July and August when all the snow is mostly gone, the wildflowers are in full bloom and the historic Rim Drive is open. This 33-mile route is the easiest and most popular way to see the national park. It should take up to 40 minutes to complete the drive if you don't stop.

But you will stop, because beneath the serene dark blue waters sits a dormant volcano that literally blew its top more than 7,700 years ago, leaving behind the caldera we now see today.

Over time, lava cooled and sealed the bottom. Rain and snow melt filled the caldera with pristine and fresh water, creating the 1,943-foot-deep lake. The depth and clarity explain why the color of the lake is one of its most noteworthy attributes. As sunlight penetrates the lake, it absorbs all the colors of visible light except for blue, which it reflects back. The deeper and clearer the water, the more magnificent the reflected blue becomes. The hue is so unique that it is referred to as Crater Lake blue.

As you make your way around the lake, get peekaboo views of Wizard Island and Phantom Ship Island. There are a few places to see wildflower fields, too. You could easily spend the day on this leisurely drive. If you'd rather someone else take the wheel, hop on the Crater Lake Trolley, which makes

Historic Crater Lake Lodge is a landmark, charming visitors since 1915.

POINTS OF INTEREST

FUN FACTS

Crater Lake itself is 6 miles wide. It is the deepest body of fresh water in the U.S. with a depth of 1,943 feet.

WORDS TO THE WISE

Daybreak, when a remarkable shade of blue reflects from the water's surface, is the best time to see the lake.

There are two campgrounds, at Mazama and at Lost Creek, both accessible by road from Rim Drive. They are only open in the summer. With a permit you can camp in the backcountry.

Crater Lake is particularly beautiful in winter and, despite an annual snowfall of 533 inches, easy to visit. The road is kept clear, and a ski trail circles the crater rim. On weekends from Thanksgiving to April, you can join snowshoe hikes led by a park ranger.

up to seven stops along its two-hour tour of Rim Drive. Plus, a ranger is on board to share trivia and fun facts about the park.

Some visitors want more than a jaunt around the rim. These folks lace up their boots and trek the park's 90 miles of trails. Ranging from easy to challenging, these paths lead to amazing views.

Pinnacles Trail will have you thinking you are in the Badlands of South Dakota. In this truly unique geologic area, the spear-shaped pinnacles formed when hot ash cooled after the big eruption.

Watchman Peak Trail takes you to a fire lookout above Wizard Island, which is known as one of the best spots in the park to watch the sunset.

The rocky climb of the Garfield Peak Trail winds past wildflowers and unusual vegetation. You might even spot a marmot or two. If you are up for a bit of a more adventurous hike, consider the one to Mount Scott, the highest peak in the park. The 4.5-mile round-trip hike is best undertaken in the early morning hours. Another sunrise sensation is Discovery Point Trail. The breathtaking views of a blue sky filled with displays of orange and red are your visual reward for getting up before dawn.

Just one trail actually leads to the water's edge—the Cleetwood Cove Trail. It is moderately steep, but only about 2.2 miles long. Cleetwood Cove is the only shoreline where swimmers can enter the lake. The water is about 57 degrees in summer, so be prepared for a chilly reception.

If you'd rather not wade into the water or take a summertime version of a polar plunge, set sail on a boat tour of the lake. Eight tours depart Cleetwood Cove daily. There are a couple of options: a two-hour trip that will take you around the caldera or a longer trip that includes a stop at Wizard Island (the boat tour is the only way to get there). The latter gives visitors a chance to swim and explore the island, which is actually a cinder cone formed during later eruptions. It's a terrific outing for kids because they can experience one of the lake's standout volcanic features.

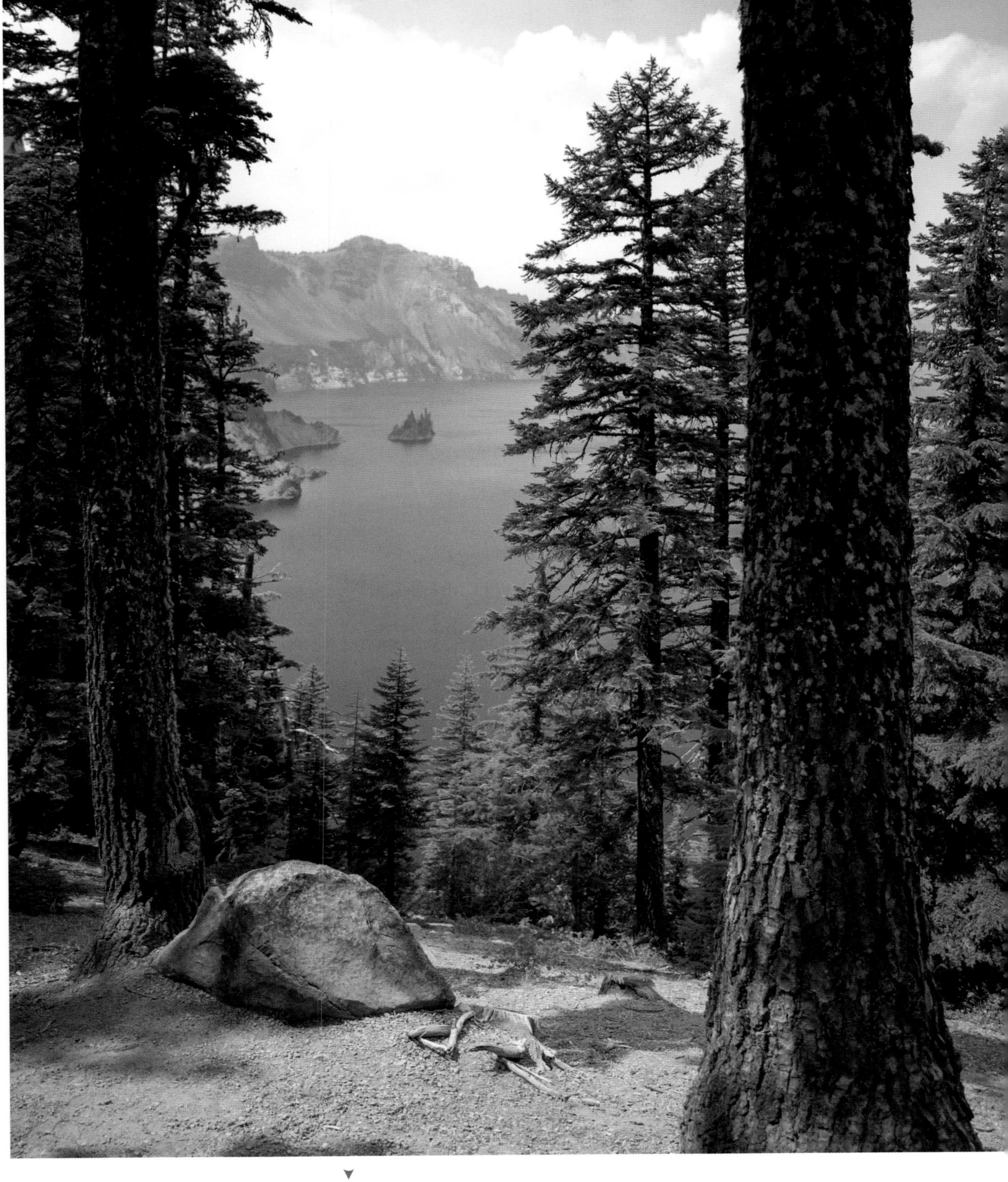

▼
Phantom Ship Island is a natural rock formation found within Crater Lake.

▼
Rubber rabbitbrush, a popular snack with deer, blooms on the rim of Crater Lake.

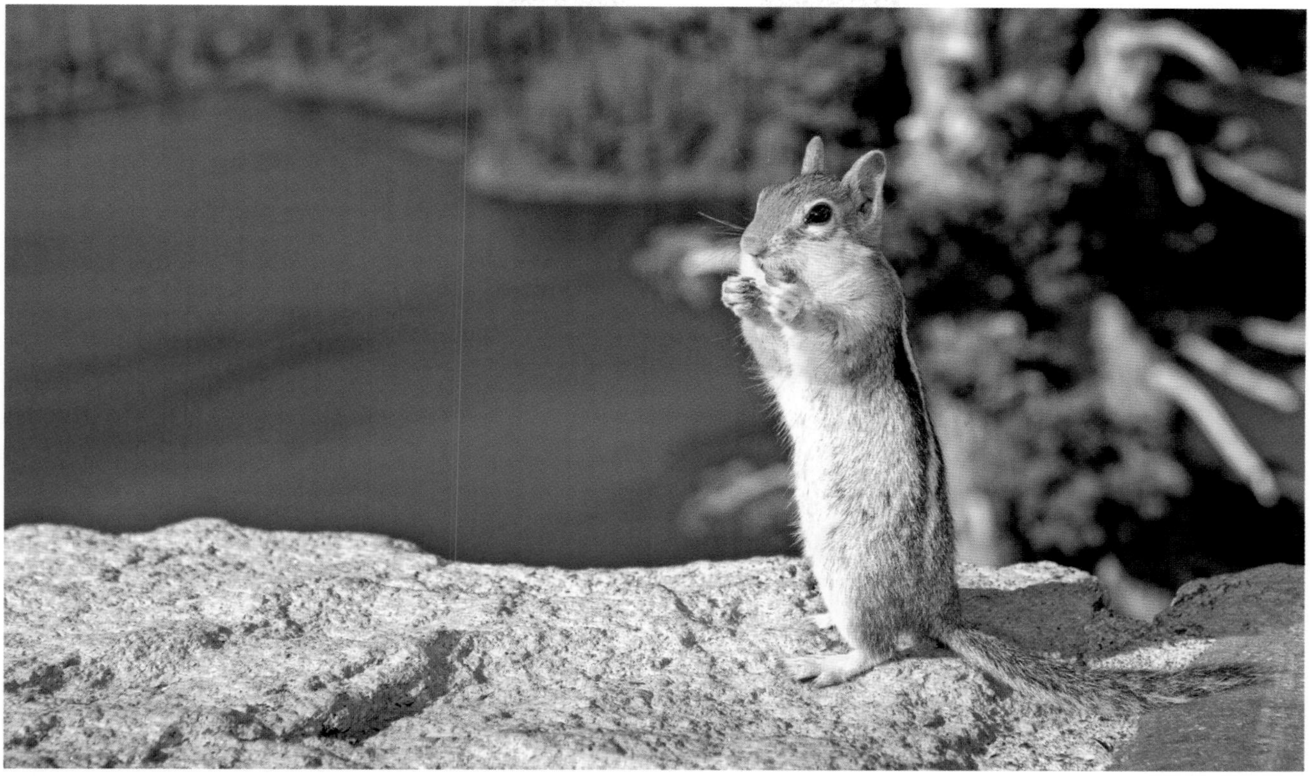

▼
A golden-mantled ground squirrel nibbles on an almond.

Crater Lake and its surrounding forest filled with mountain hemlock and pine are home to an abundance of birds. Spot eagles and peregrine falcons along the rim cliffs or look for American dippers near streams. Wildfire-burned forests attract several species of woodpeckers, including the rare black-backed and three-toed woodpeckers. Common mergansers can be seen on the lake, and calls of songbirds permeate the forests and the meadows.

Mammal sightings are far less common, but a wide variety of animals inhabit the terrain around the lake, including bobcats, gray wolves, red foxes, cougars and several species of marten, to name but a few. Expect to encounter several white-tailed deer, since they seem oblivious to visitors.

Even if you opt to stay outside the park or in a campground, don't miss a visit to historic Crater Lake Lodge. Originally opened in 1915, the lodge takes you back to the rustic charm of the 1920s. If you do choose to stay, it is an experience you will never forget.

Located on the edge of the caldera and overlooking the lake, the lodge has fantastic views of this natural wonder. Rise with the sun in the morning and eat a hearty breakfast before heading out to the trails, or upon your return refuel with an elegant dinner and sip a glass of wine in the dining room.

As a landscape photographer, I have always been drawn to Crater Lake. I was delighted that my daughter Nicki recognized its beauty so many years ago. Although I don't know if our trip planted some kind of seed, today she is a landscape photographer, too. Crater Lake is truly a magical place. ●

▼
The stunning view from Green River Overlook.

STORY AND PHOTOS BY
TIM FITZHARRIS

CANYONLANDS

A MAJESTIC DESERT MARVEL RICHLY REWARDS TRAVELERS WHO HAVE THE GUMPTION AND FOUR-WHEEL DRIVE.

THE DRAMATIC VISTAS at Canyonlands National Park rival those of the Grand Canyon, while its exotic geology is first cousin to that of a nearby and better-known national park, Arches.

I've spent many very thrilling days chasing endless photo opportunities in this immense region of deep canyons, sheer-drop mesas, staircase benchlands and soaring sandstone spires.

A remote high-desert wilderness, with elevations ranging from 3,700 to 7,200 feet above sea level, Canyonlands is one of my favorite places to shoot Wild West landscapes.

The park sprawls over 337,598 sparsely populated acres in southeast Utah, not far from the town of Moab.

It is composed of three sections whose boundaries are loosely carved by the Colorado and Green rivers. The three sections are isolated from one another, and you reach them by separate dead-end roads that snake inward from the park periphery.

The Needles district is on the southeast side of the Colorado River, about 90 minutes from Moab. This is the most developed part of the park, with a small store, cafe, visitor center and campground.

Needles, named for the area's vibrantly colored sandstone spires, is also known for its steep canyons, towering arches and buttes.

Visitors can explore more than 60 miles of interconnecting trails, which can be challenging even for experienced hikers, or about 50 miles of backcountry roads for those in a four-wheel-drive vehicle. The incredible scenery is worth the extra effort.

Looming over the northern reaches of the park, Island in the Sky is a grand, flat-topped, tree-studded mesa about 45 minutes from Moab.

It's the easiest area of the park for visitors to reach and the best location for capturing those fabulous panoramic shots. A meandering paved road connects numerous overlooks of the river-carved terrain thousands of feet below. Facilities include a visitor center and small campground.

I love to spend the early morning in this part of the park hiking several of

Mesa Arch, in the Island in the Sky region, offers fantastic sunrises.

POINTS OF INTEREST

FUN FACTS

Canyonlands is the largest yet the least developed of the national parks located in Utah.

Historic people of many cultures have visited the area over a span lasting more than 10,000 years—relying on and exploiting the rich resources that hide in the desert landscape. Many prehistoric campsites exist within the park's boundaries.

You'll find short trails leading to an ancient Anasazi granary and to an abandoned cowboy's camp that features century-old wooden and iron handmade furnishings.

SIDE TRIP

If you have time to venture outside the park on a brief side trip, you won't want to miss the dramatic view of Canyonlands from the adjacent Dead Horse Point State Park.

the short trails to discover how the light is mottling the exotic rock forms carved by the river.

The Shafer Trail Road leaves the mesa's rim and drops 1,000 feet in a series of jaw-clenching switchbacks to the White Rim, a massive bench of rock that encircles Island in the Sky.

The Maze district is Canyonlands' least-visited sector, and thorough preparation is a must before mounting any expedition there.

This labyrinth of multihued rock canyons is accessible only by four-wheel drive or by hiking over remote unmarked trails.

I have not ventured into the Maze, but this trek is high on my wish list, along with spotting and photographing the park's elusive desert bighorn sheep and mountain lions.

Spring, with its pleasant weather, light crowds and burst of wildflower color, is my favorite time to visit Canyonlands. Typically, daytime highs reach a comfortable 60 to 80 degrees.

May and early June offer flowering cacti and herbs, which I photograph on rare overcast days, when the landscapes lose some of their drama to the soft light.

Summer's high temperatures, frequently exceeding 100 degrees, make hiking difficult. But the heat also stirs up thunderstorms that add rainbows, magnificent sunsets and clouds of all shapes and colors to an already sumptuous array.

In autumn, aspens and cottonwoods along the rivers and streams put on a nice show of fall color, made even more enjoyable by clear October skies and pleasant temperatures.

I've also tested my cameras here in the winter, when snow dusts the tawny or rusty wilderness. Use caution when visiting during winter, however, as even a light snowfall can make roads treacherous to navigate.

Through the lens, and to my eyes, Canyonlands' raw, undisturbed beauty is remarkable all year-round.

Washer Woman Arch, in the distance here, looks just like its name states.

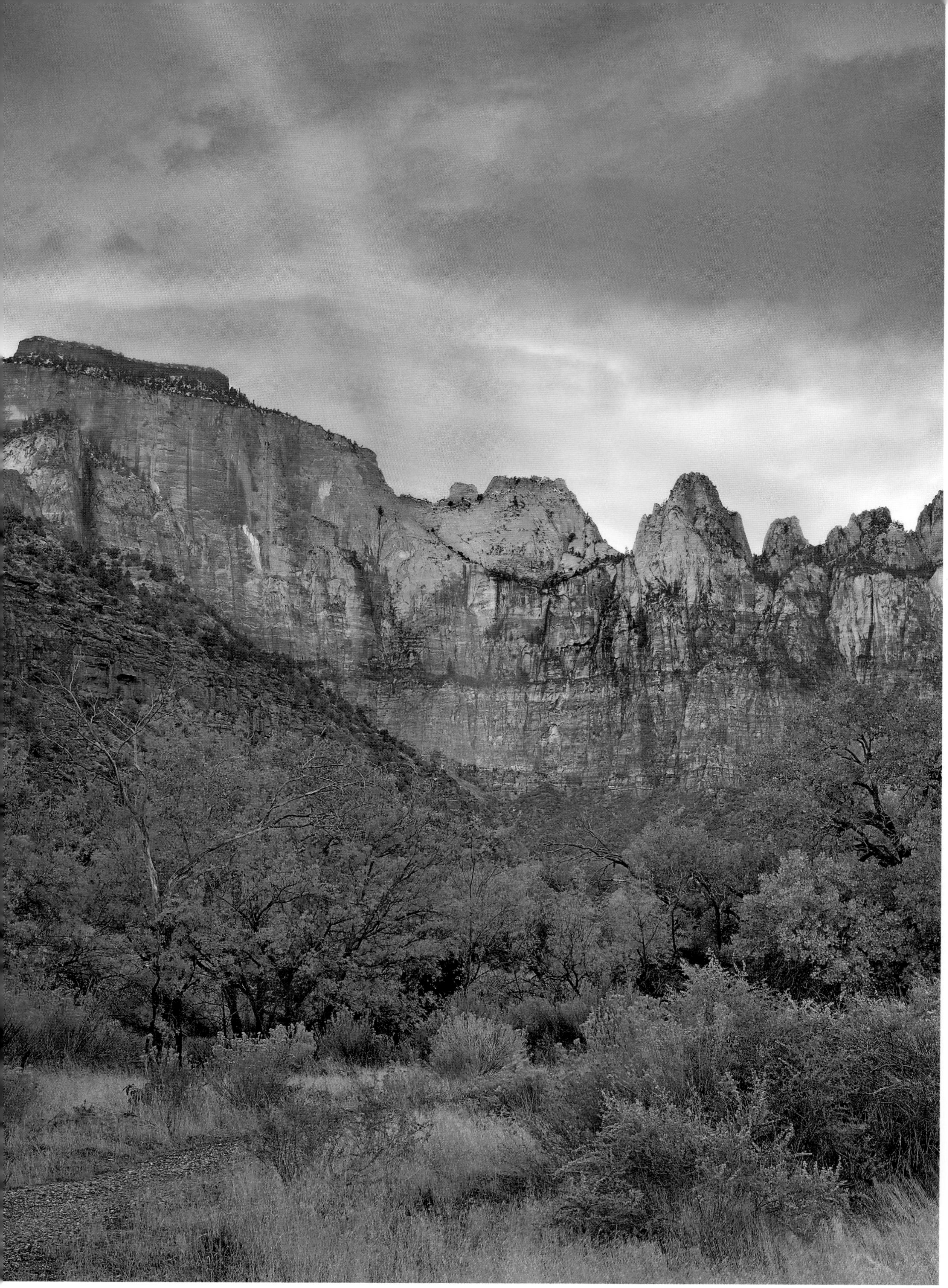

▼
An early morning rainbow appears at the Towers of the Virgin.

STORY AND PHOTOS BY
TIM FITZHARRIS

ZION

WIND YOUR WAY THROUGH VIBRANT SANDSTONE MOUNTAINS, COTTONWOODS AND THE GLORIOUS VIRGIN RIVER.

THE ZION-MOUNT CARMEL HIGHWAY, a section of Utah's Scenic Byway 9, can be driven in less than 45 minutes, yet it draws some 3 million visitors yearly from all parts of the globe. You could spend months exploring the grand mountain and desert attractions that are peppered along the route. It is the main thoroughfare through Zion National Park and connects to the prime tourist draw of the region—Zion Canyon Scenic Drive. That drive follows the Virgin River northward through Zion Canyon to the Temple of Sinawava, an elegant 2,000-foot-high sandstone rampart with delicate groves of cottonwood and box elder interlaced around its feet.

It was 30 years ago that I first became intrigued with the area as I sat at my kitchen table planning my first photo trip into southern Utah's red rock country. Names on this part of the map seemed a little overblown: Great White Throne, Angel's Landing and Checkerboard Mesa, to mention a few. Apparently, the area made quite an impression on the European settlers.

Once I arrived, I had to admit I was mistaken. These names understate the majesty of these natural monuments. It's not just the colors (vermillion, rust, buff, ochre) but the immense scale, which tends to get muffled by its own grandeur until a raven passes high overhead, a black speck against the

▼
These cottonwood trees hug the Virgin River.

POINTS OF INTEREST

FUN FACT
As the sun sets, photography becomes a social event for Zion visitors. You'll find fellow shutterbugs on the Pa'rus Trail happily snapping an iconic shot of The Watchman. Capturing Bridge Mountain is as easy as visiting the Zion Human History Museum and turning your camera east.

WORDS TO THE WISE
Even if you're just driving through, you'll need to pay the full park entrance fees. Also, the route's 1.1-mile tunnel requires a permit for big vehicles like motor homes. And from March to October, access to the 6-mile Zion Canyon Scenic Drive spur is by shuttle bus only. In winter, you're allowed to drive your own car.

red, which rises another thousand feet, perhaps, into the blue.

There are more than just natural marvels here. The Zion-Mount Carmel Highway is an engineering wonder in itself. It is listed in the National Register of Historic Places and designated as a Historic Civil Engineering Landmark. Construction was completed in 1930 as part of the Grand Circle Tour connecting southwest Utah's scenic spots with the north rim of the Grand Canyon in a quicker, easier route to lure visitors.

Photogenic views are stacked up in every direction, and I want to shoot them all right away. But eventually, I calm down enough to park, get out the camera and tripod and proceed on foot. Surprisingly, walking among these sandstone colossi (among the largest anywhere) seems as cinematic as viewing them at highway speed. The near-vertical walls, though enormous, are so tightly packed, so close, so varied in form and color that new compositions pass my eyes at a steady clip. I set up the tripod, frame a chiseled chasm that glows intensely red under reflected sunlight and then pad another hundred feet through river sand before I stop and do it again. This time, cottonwoods gracefully outline an opening in the canyon, which reveals another stone amphitheater within—dim, mysterious, inviting. When my shutter clicks, a mule deer raises its head from a brushy gold chamisa shrub nearby. A small flock of wild turkeys continues to forage, unconcerned except for a pair of toms that shake and fluff their formidable feathers into a courtship display. Zion National Park is home to an abundant variety of birds, mammals, amphibians and reptiles. Except for the latter—I spy many types of lizards basking in the hot midday rays—it seems that most of the inhabitants hunker down in shady places to keep cool.

The area's plant life is equally diverse, ranging from wetlands to arid grasslands to coniferous forest high up on sandstone crevices. How can a total of 900 different plant species exist here? The drastic changes in elevation, ranging from 3,600 to 8,700 feet, create multiple microhabitats in the park.

The river's murmur sets a soothing pace as I move past each new scene, each picture feeling different from the one before. The light changes, and cottonwoods photographed earlier along the Virgin River glow green compared to their muted cousins photographed at the foot of Bridge Mountain as the sky grows dark. As the color drops out of the canyon, I know it's time to call it a day. But I will be back along the road tomorrow, just as I will be next year and the year after. Why stop after three decades? The seasons and sunlight guarantee fresh perspectives. The excitement never fades. ■

Prickly pear cactuses mimic Zion's iconic mountains.

STORY BY
CAROL PUCCI

MOUNT RAINIER

EACH WINTER, ALMOST 600 INCHES OF POWDER FALLS IN THIS NATIONAL PARK, MAKING IT A PERFECT SNOW PLAYGROUND.

WHEN YOU VISIT Mount Rainier National Park, you will see splendid meadows of wildflowers give way to thick blankets of snow at the Paradise visitors area that sits at an elevation of 5,400 feet. Winter draws campers, hikers and snowshoers into wilderness areas like the Mazama Ridge, where white powder covers alpine meadows and crystalline frost coats the trees. Stunning views of the mountain reward downhill skiers at nearby Crystal Mountain Resort, nestled in the Cascade Range, a few miles from the park's northeastern entrance.

Named for the mirror views of Mount Rainier reflected in its subalpine lakes, the Reflection Lakes area attracts snowshoers and cross-country skiers to the edges of what look like frozen meadows in winter. Glissading—sliding downhill on one's feet or buttocks—is a fast and fun way to descend slopes here.

One of the few species of wildlife you might spot that thrives in winter at the park's higher elevations is the Cascade red fox. They have tails with white tips, and their legs are black.

And though snow falls early at Mount Rainier—blanketing meadows with deep drifts that can cover the ground into June—you may also find dark blue and black Steller's jays, along with crows and ravens.

Climbers use Emmons Glacier as a route to reach the summit of Mount Rainier. In winter, mountaineers believe it receives some of the best powder for backcountry skiing.

Though amazing all year, the park is a winter snow lover's dream.

Top: A camper looks on at Mount Rainier in the distance from Mazama Ridge. Bottom: The ski lift at Crystal Mountain Resort.

TOP: IMAGES BY T.O.K./ALAMY STOCK PHOTO; BOTTOM: DESIGN PICS/STUART WESTMORLAND/GETTY IMAGES

POINTS OF INTEREST

FUN FACT

Mount Rainier National Park's premier attractions—Longmire, Paradise, the Grove of the Patriarchs and Sunrise—are all linked by a single winding road that enters the park at its southwestern corner.

WORDS TO THE WISE

Visit in summer for wildflowers, early fall for foliage and fewer crowds, and in winter for snow fun. From November to April all park roads except the Nisqually-Paradise road are usually closed.

NEARBY ATTRACTION

For a close encounter with Mount St. Helens, the explosive neighbor of Mount Rainier that blew its top in 1980 and began erupting again in 2004, head south on Highway 12 to Randle along the White Pass Scenic Byway. Take S.R. 131, which leads to Forest Service roads 25 and 99, where visitors can stop for breathtaking pictures of St. Helens' crater from Windy Ridge. This route is only open in the summer months, but the views are certainly worth the wait.

STORY BY
DANA MEREDITH

NORTH CASCADES

ALPINE JOY WITH LESS OF THE BUSYNESS FOUND IN OTHER NATIONAL PARKS MAKES FOR A PEACEFUL EXPERIENCE.

WITH FEW VISITORS, it's an easy choice to seek out the crystal clear glacial lakes, rugged mountains and gorgeous landscapes about three hours north of Seattle along North Cascades Highway (state Route 20). The road cuts across 684,237 acres of the North Cascades National Park Service Complex. This area stretches from the Canadian border through the Ross Lake National Recreation Area to Lake Chelan.

Start at North Cascades Visitor Center near Newhalem and drive east for captivating scenic overlooks, hiking trails of varying levels, campgrounds, climbing areas and riding trails. Take an easy hike to Ladder Creek Falls or a short walk on the fully accessible Sterling Munro Viewpoint Trail to see dramatic views of the remote Picket Range. And don't miss Diablo Lake.

The park's diverse ecosystem is home to elusive mammals such as the gray wolf, at least 28 species of fish and more than 200 bird species. In addition, 260 archaeological sites have been identified—some older than 8,500 years—including mining camps, fire lookouts and sheep herder camps. Scenery, wildlife, history and recreation—North Cascades National Park has it all. ■

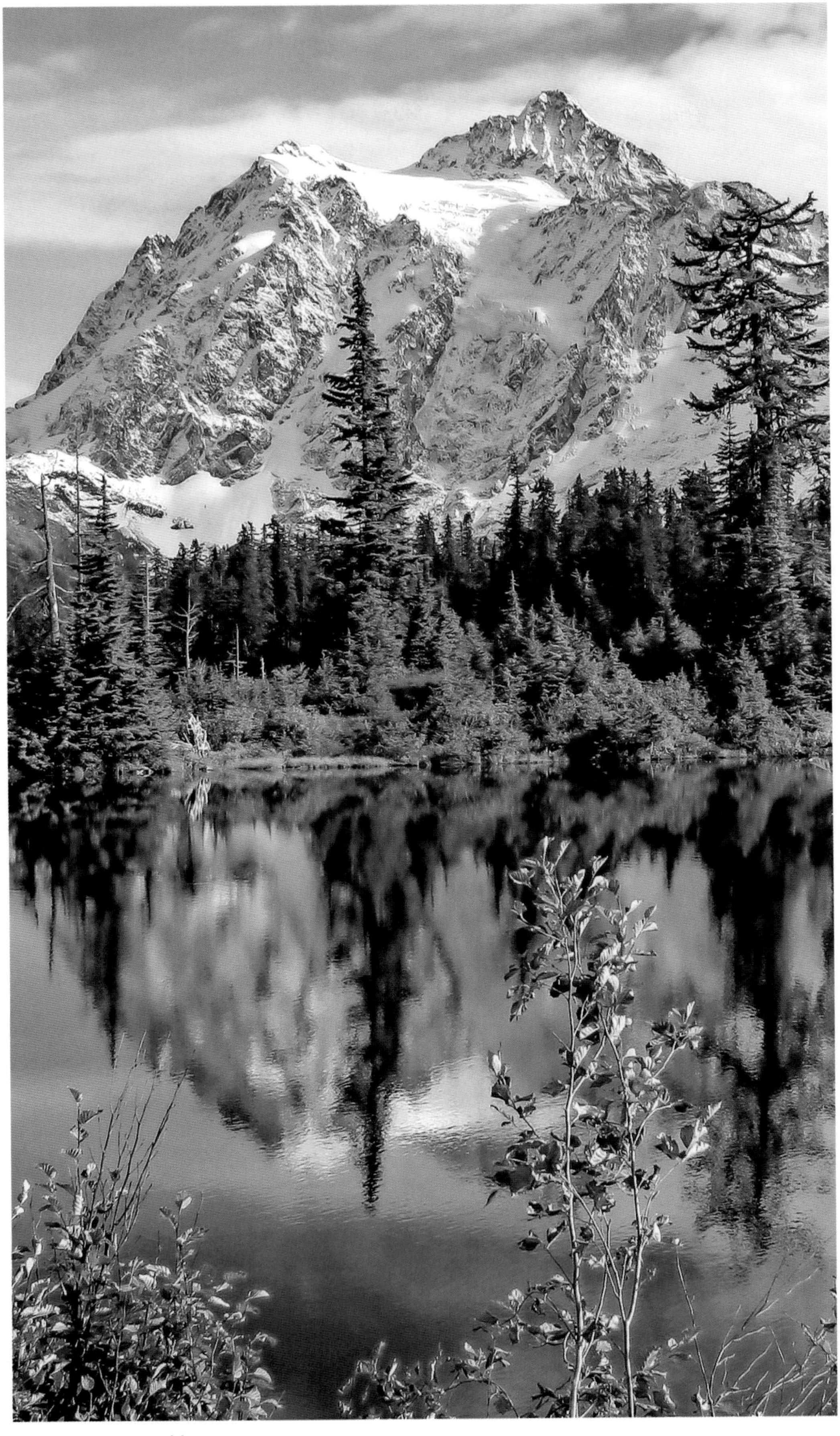

MADHULIKA SARUPRIA/GETTY IMAGES

Rising more than 9,000 feet, Mount Shuksan overlooks pristine Picture Lake.

POINTS OF INTEREST

NOT TO BE MISSED

Ladder Creek Falls is lovely and definitely worth the stop. And you will get some of your best views in the park at Diablo Lake Overlook and Washington Pass Overlook.

The beautiful Skagit Valley Tulip Festival is held in April every year.

WORDS TO THE WISE

Plan to visit between mid-June to October.

Be aware that no fuel is available on the 70-mile stretch of S.R. 20 between Marblemount and Mazama.

NEARBY ATTRACTIONS

San Juan Islands (via ferry from Anacortes); Space Needle, Seattle.

JUAN MARIA COY VERGARA/GETTY IMAGES

▼
Sol Duc Falls is surrounded by a forest of 200-year-old hemlock trees.

STORY BY
LESLIE FORSBERG

OLYMPIC

WITH LUSH FORESTS, WATERFALLS AND SANDY BEACHES, THIS DRIVE IS FOR NATURE LOVERS.

CHLOROPHYLL RULES in the damp Pacific Northwest. Experience it firsthand on a drive around Washington state's Olympic Peninsula loop, where logging trucks have given way to SUVs loaded with bikes and kayaks. You'll easily see the green in the Hoh Rain Forest, where bigleaf maples stoop like old men under the weight of thick pads of mosses and epiphytes (plants that grow on other plants for support). And you can almost taste it in the salt-tinged air of the area's pristine Pacific shore, where hemlock and red cedar forests trail down to beaches pounded by ocean waves.

With high mountain peaks, dense forests and ocean beaches, Olympic National Park—an UNESCO World Heritage Site—is the heart of the peninsula. It's flanked on three sides by Highway 101, which ribbons through small towns on a loop drive of more than 300 miles.

When you first lay your eyes on the peninsula, it will likely be from Seattle. From there, the snow-tipped Olympic Range forms a jagged outline on the western horizon. You'll aim straight for those peaks on board a Washington State Ferry from downtown Seattle to Bainbridge Island, an exciting start.

Make Port Townsend your first stop. This historic seaport features a fleet of painted ladies—beautifully restored and painted Victorian homes. Its downtown is filled with boutiques in old brick buildings. On its northern flank, Fort Worden Historical State Park is the site of year-round arts and culture festivals, and its lovely sand beach is marked by the 1914 Point Wilson Lighthouse.

After rounding a couple of tranquil bays, you'll arrive at the lavender capital of North America: Sequim. Spring and summer bring sweet scents to visitors strolling the grounds of the area's lavender farms. Many of the farms have gift shops where you can buy elixirs, potions and culinary items made from the fragrant herb.

Port Angeles, the largest town on the peninsula, is the gateway to Olympic National Park and a good spot to pull

POINTS OF INTEREST

NOT TO BE MISSED
Roll along the Olympic Discovery Trail, a bike path that goes past farmland, forest and ocean.

FUN FACT
Olympic National Park protects the largest unmanaged herd of Roosevelt elk in the world. Olympic was almost named "Elk National Park" and was established in part to protect these stately animals.

WORDS TO THE WISE
Bring adequate rain gear for hiking and camping. When beach walking, consult a tide table.

SIDE TRIPS
Watch wildlife at Dungeness Spit Recreation Area, home of the nation's longest natural sand spit at 5.5 miles. The spit is part of the Dungeness National Wildlife Refuge, which lies on the Pacific Flyway.

Paddle out of Freshwater Bay to sea caves and harbor seal haul-outs with Adventures Through Kayaking. Rent equipment or take a guided tour.

▼
Kayaks rest on the shore of Lake Crescent in Olympic National Park.

in for the night and have a leisurely dinner. Next Door Gastropub, known for using fresh and local ingredients, is one of my favorite establishments.

Just beyond town, kick into low gear for the 17-mile climb to the 5,242-foot Hurricane Ridge. Here you'll experience jaw-dropping vistas of glaciated mountains. Alpine meadows are the home of black-tailed deer and Olympic marmots—adorably chubby rodents with shrill whistles.

Farther west, Highway 101 hugs the curves of the 12-mile-long Lake Crescent, whose cobalt depths are legendary. Also sparking stories is Lake Crescent Lodge, an arts-and-crafts-style resort perched on the shoreline. Some say President Franklin Roosevelt's overnight stay here in 1937 played a role in the creation of Olympic National Park.

Across the highway, a short hike leads to Marymere Falls, a 90-foot cascade in a rock alcove draped with delicate maidenhair ferns. Just a few miles farther, the Sol Duc Hot Springs beckon with relaxing thermal soaking pools and a spectacular nature walk through a mossy old-growth forest to Sol Duc Falls.

Just past the former timber town of Forks, the Hoh Rain Forest owes its existence to moisture-laden weather systems rolling off the Pacific that drop an average of 12 feet of rain annually. You see the rain's effect along the Hall of Mosses nature trail, where you will find massive, primeval trees covered with moss, and every square foot hosts an exuberant tangle of plant life.

Highway 101 finally reaches the Pacific at Ruby Beach, one of the crown jewels of Olympic National Park. The sensory experience here is full-on, with the tang of salt air, sea gulls mewling over the roar of the ocean and a broad sandy beach to sink your toes into. It's a visual feast as well, as seabirds swirl about sentinel-like sea stacks and brilliant anemones and sea stars glisten at the bottom of tide pools. The sun-bleached driftwood piled high is just one more reminder of the vast forests on this verdant thumb of land jutting into the Pacific Ocean. ■

LEFT: YINYANG/GETTY IMAGES; RIGHT: DAVE LOGAN

▼ *The trail to the top of Mount Angeles has steep switchbacks through meadows of flowers and fresh alpine air.*

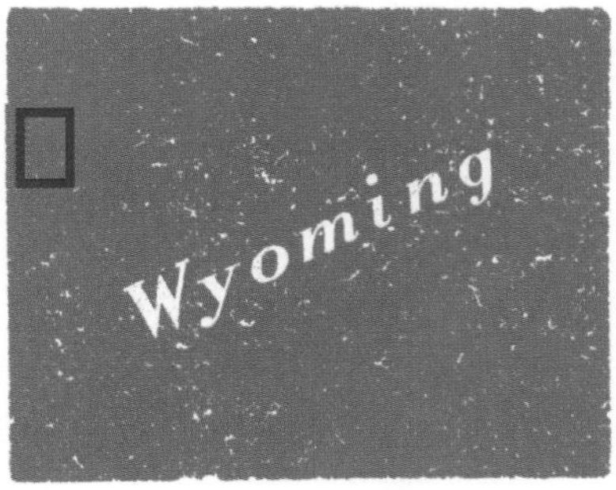

STORY BY
TIM FITZHARRIS

GRAND TETON

MULTIPLE TURNOUTS, OVERLOOKS AND TRAILS REVEAL THE GRANDEUR OF SOARING PEAKS AND MOUNTAIN LAKES.

NO TERRAIN IN AMERICA'S Lower 48 states surpasses the Grand Tetons for sheer eye-popping splendor. The upward thrust of these ice-crowned peaks, rising abruptly from surrounding prairies, is simultaneously inspiring and soulful. You feel good being around them.

The Tetons lord over their territory like abiding grandfathers. And at their base is a flurry of activity—tourists aplenty, but this place is preserved for moose, elk, bison, bear, coyote, squirrels, chipmunks, eagles and owls that confidently roam Wyoming's Grand Teton National Park.

Teton Park Road, a 43-mile loop drive, winds through lakes, forests and meadows as it snuggles against the mountain foothills. Highway 26/89/191 completes the circle and provides a more distant perspective on Teton grandeur. Branch off on Schwabacher Landing Road for an iconic photo at Schwabacher Landing.

The warmer seasons are my favorites for circling the Tetons. In spring and summer, the fields of wildflowers—particularly brazen patches of lupines and sunflowers—and newborn bison, elk and moose are what lure me to photograph here. You can snap them from your car window or hike into the fields (avoid meadows with bison to avoid being the target of a charge).

Autumn is when the elk and moose are in rut and antlered champions beg for challengers. I use a telephoto lens to keep my distance from these bulls—an unpredictable but thrilling bunch.

I like to alternate these gripping sessions with quiet work along the shores of String and Leigh lakes or Oxbow Bend, where still waters catch the reflection of Mount Moran or Grand Teton warmed by a rising sun. Fall is also aspen season, and the lower slopes and watercourses flash gold and bronze tints.

The meandering route through the park is peppered with wildlife, historic ranch buildings and grand views, and the trip never disappoints. ■

Top: A route into the magical lands between the mountains and beyond. Bottom: Bison are sturdy icons at Antelope Flats.

TOP: PETER MANGOLDS; BOTTOM: TIM FITZHARRIS

POINTS OF INTEREST

NOT TO BE MISSED

Take Jenny Lake Scenic Drive off Teton Park Road for a spectacular view of the peaks. While there, don't miss Hidden Falls and Inspiration Point.

FUN FACT

In the very heart of Grand Teton National Park, Jenny Lake formed from melted glaciers about 60,000 years ago.

NEARBY ATTRACTIONS

Fossil Butte National Monument, WY, (fossil displays); Lava Hot Springs, ID, (known for its hot mineral pools); Periodic Spring, WY, (the spring gushes every 18 minutes from an opening in a canyon wall); Bridger-Teton National Forest, WY.

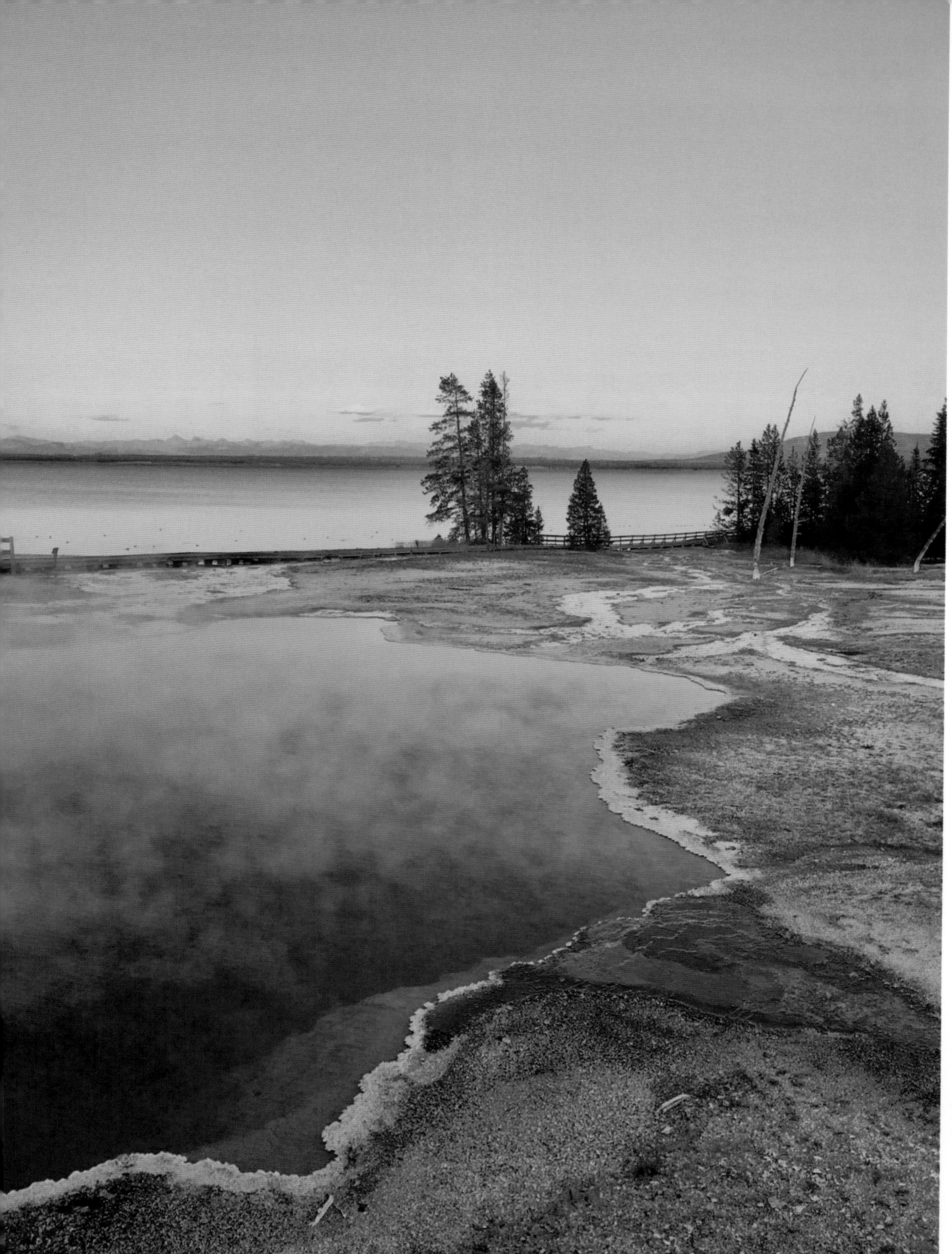

SYNDY DOWLING

▼
In the early evening, steam seems to drift endlessly from the West Thumb Geyser Basin.

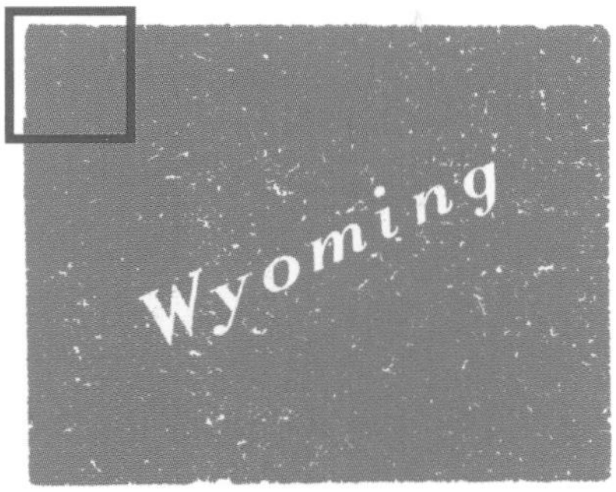

STORY BY
PEGGY KONZACK

YELLOWSTONE

THERE WAS GOOD REASON TO GO THEN, AND SO MANY AMAZING REASONS TO COME BACK TO MAKE MEMORIES.

I HAVE SO MANY FOND REMEMBRANCES of Yellowstone National Park that I feel as if I grew up there.

In the late 1920s and '30s my family lived in Butte, Montana, where my father owned a grocery store. We traveled to the park each summer. I remember one holiday weekend we spent in Yellowstone. I was 10 years old and excited to see my first geyser coming out of the side of the banks of the Firehole River. It wasn't long before we saw Emerald Pool, Morning Glory Pool and the (at the time) famous Handkerchief Pool, where a hankie would disappear and then reappear a few seconds later much cleaner and whiter. Unfortunately, people put so many things in the pool the debris damaged the "plumbing." Now the pool is all but forgotten.

Our next stop was the Old Faithful Inn to reserve a cabin for the night. Our cabin was simple and clean with two double beds separated by a curtain. We spent our evening listening to the park rangers lecture at the outdoor amphitheater, all the time watching and waiting for a bear to walk by.

At 6 the next morning we heard a knock on the door, and it opened (there were no locks on the doors). A young man declared "fire boy" and came in to build our fire. It took about three minutes and soon we had a cozy, warm room (he used a mixture of sawdust and coal oil to get the fire going in a hurry).

After the thrill of watching the famous geyser Old Faithful, we saw the thick, gray and bubbly mudpots, or mud pools. How they did smell like rotten eggs!

Then we headed to the Canyon Hotel (which is no longer), to reserve a cabin, and we received the same hospitality as we did at the Inn.

After a hearty breakfast the next day, we headed to Uncle Tom's Trail to walk to the bottom of Lower Falls. We walked down 900 steps, as I recall. Going down was fairly easy, but going

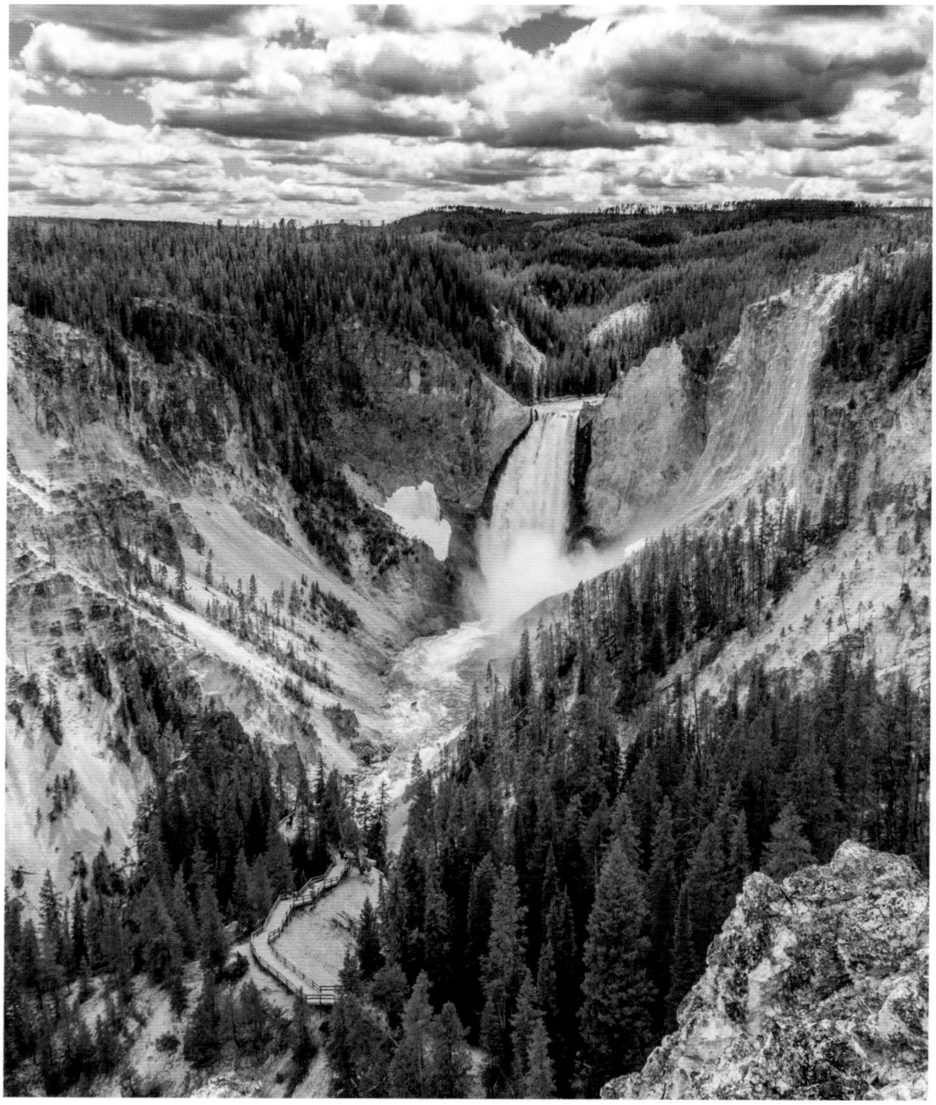

▼
Lower Falls is by far the most popular waterfall in the park.

FUN FACTS
Some geologists believe that the Norris Geyser Basin, named after a former superintendent of Yellowstone, may be the hottest place on Earth.

The floor of Yellowstone's Hayden Valley is covered with clay and lake sediments left from the most recent glacial retreat, 13,000 years ago, which is why the area is mostly marsh and lacks any trees.

WORDS TO THE WISE
Food, fuel and lodging are available at Canyon Village, Grant Village, Mammoth Hot Springs and Old Faithful.

Most park roads are closed from November through April, but park snowmobiles can be rented in winter.

NEARBY ATTRACTIONS
Beartooth Highway (Route 212); Grand Teton National Park.

back up we made use of the landing at every 50 steps and rested on a bench. It was quite a good feeling to accomplish such a great hike.

We then drove to Mammoth Hot Springs, which at that time was a very beautiful sight. Of course, those older than me had to visit Devil's Kitchen, a dried-up spring that the park service closed after discovering that carbon dioxide sometimes filled it. It was a scary place for a child.

Driving through the gate in Gardiner, we headed home to Butte with many happy memories of a long weekend!

Many years have passed since those visits to Yellowstone National Park. My husband and I have made six trips together. As I write this, I am in my 90s now and remember every single trip. Those were exciting and sometimes scary experiences. Summer or winter, Yellowstone is the perfect place to be out in nature. ■

Well-known Old Faithful blows off a little steam.

LEFT: KELLY CHENG TRAVEL PHOTOGRAPHY/GETTY IMAGES; RIGHT: EDWARD FIELDING/SHUTTERSTOCK

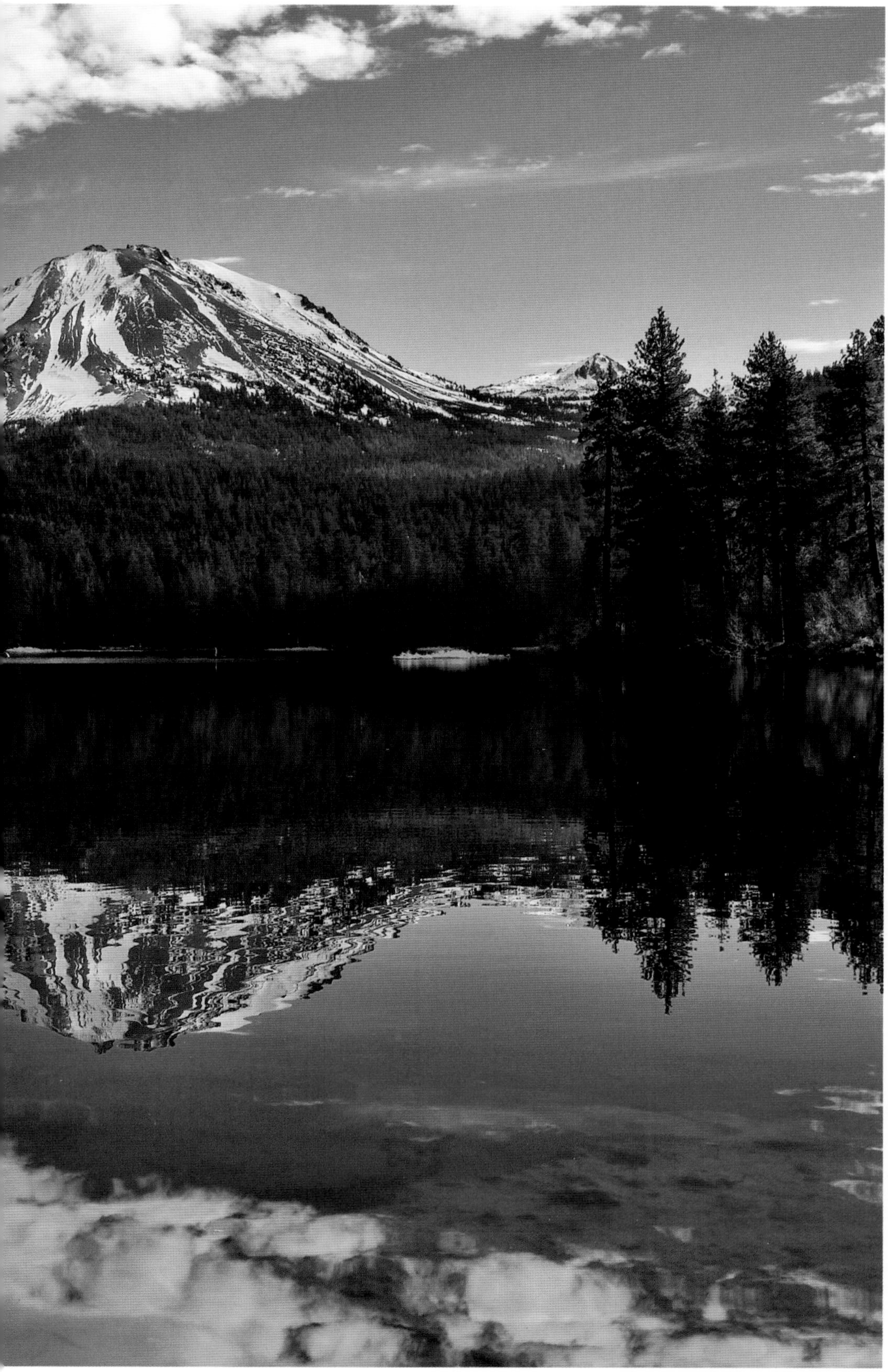

LASSEN VOLCANIC NATIONAL PARK

1934

A woman stretches as she gets ready for a swim while standing at the edge of Manzanita Lake in Lassen Volcanic National Park. Looming in the distance is Mount Lassen.

2010

You can still swim in Manzanita Lake in Lassen Volcanic National Park today, and the color photograph here shows how dazzling a reflection of Mount Lassen in its waters really can be.

THEN: GEORGE A. GRANT/U.S. NATIONAL PARK SERVICE; NOW: MBRUBIN/GETTY IMAGES

SOUTHWEST
CANYONS · DESERTS · CLIFFS

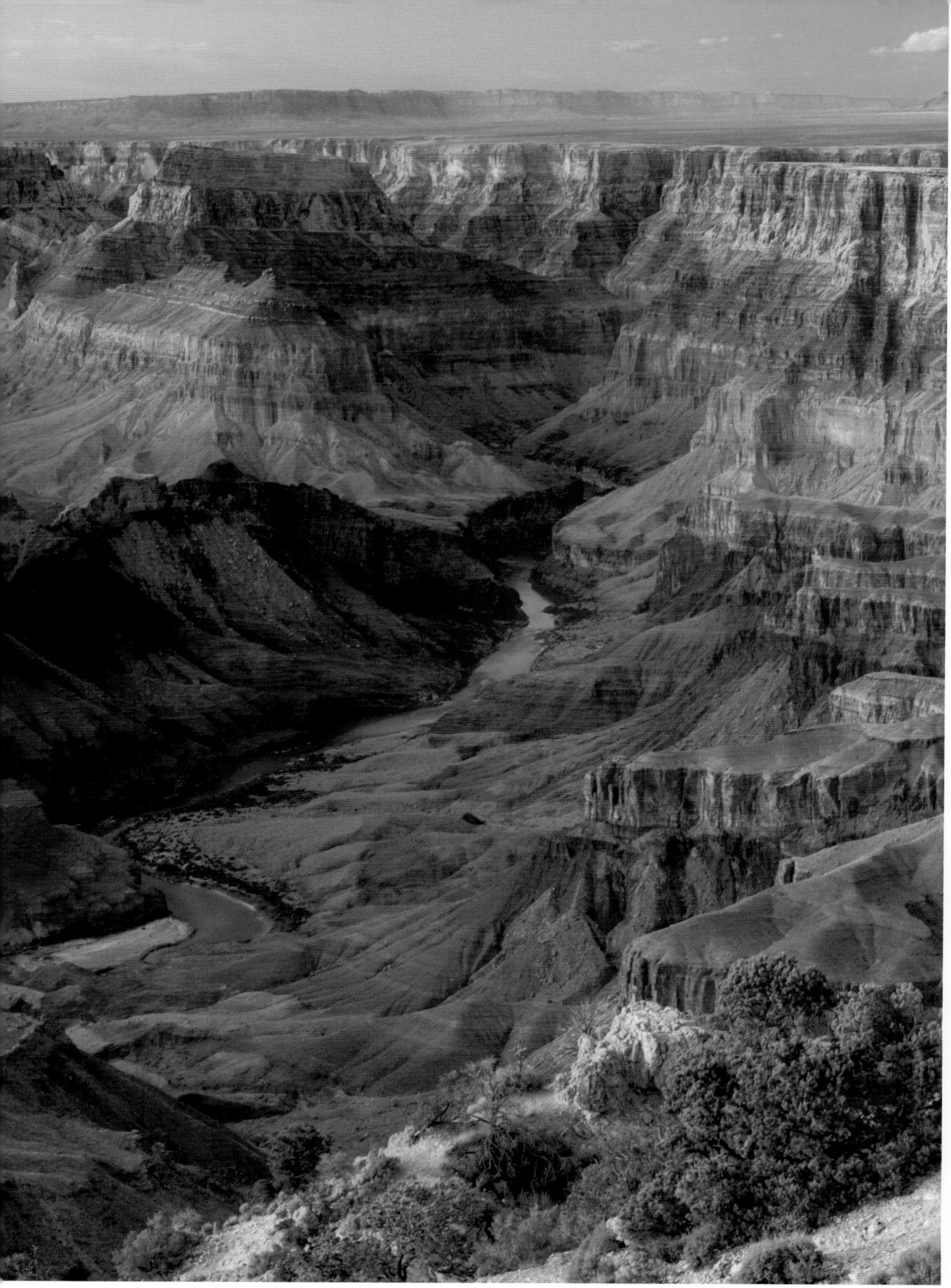

▼
A sunset paints colors on the Colorado River and the surrounding landscape deep in the Grand Canyon.

STORY AND PHOTOS BY
LORA LUCERO

GRAND CANYON

GRANDFATHER'S MOTTO, "I THINK I CAN," SPURRED THIS FIRST-TIME HIKER TO THE TOP AT THIS WELL-KNOWN SPOT.

I MADE RESERVATIONS 13 months ahead for the popular Phantom Ranch, located at the bottom of Grand Canyon National Park in Arizona. As this adventure drew near, my hiking partner canceled. Doubts crept in—could I handle a 4,860-foot elevation drop from the rim to the Colorado River, and then hike back out? A sign on the South Kaibab Trail warns hikers: Hiking down is optional; hiking back up is mandatory.

I was a newly minted senior citizen who had been to the Grand Canyon many times before, but had never hiked to the bottom by myself. If I didn't do it now, I doubted I'd get another chance.

The night before my descent, I slept like a baby at Bright Angel Lodge. I didn't have any second thoughts. I think I can do this!

The next morning, the young man at the front desk related his experience slipping and sliding down South Kaibab Trail—the one I was set to embark on! A waitress who served me a hearty breakfast at the Harvey House Cafe told me she had tried to hike down, but turned back when she realized how difficult it was. Both of them were in their late 20s or early 30s. Uh-oh!

At 8:30 a.m., I made one last check of my backpack, clicked my walking sticks together, and started down the trail.

The day was bright and sunny and the Grand Canyon looked just like any postcard I'd ever seen. The 6.3-mile South Kaibab Trail is all downhill and appeared easy to negotiate. Nearly everyone I passed asked me if I was hiking alone.

Though I took my first step solo, I never felt alone with people of all ages hiking in both directions, watching out for each other.

My naive notion of a peaceful, meditative hike was promptly discarded when I realized the trail was narrow, rocky and dangerous in many spots. Since I was one of the slowest hikers, I frequently stepped aside as others approached from both directions.

Halfway down the trail, I felt strong and confident. I certainly didn't think about turning back. The temps rose as I continued down. I peeled off layers, sipped my water and ate a protein bar.

Day hikers savor the panoramic views along the South Kaibab Trail.

POINTS OF INTEREST

WORDS TO THE WISE

If planning to hike the Grand Canyon, assume it will take you twice as long to hike out as it does to hike in.

Hike with a sturdy pair of shoes and walking sticks.

Carry a headlamp and lightweight flashlight with extra batteries and bulbs in case you end up on the trail after dark.

Bring moleskin for any blisters.

Pack an emergency blanket should temperatures drop.

Keep a whistle where you can reach it easily in case you fall.

Most important: Have drinking water with you at all times.

NEARBY ATTRACTIONS

Meteor Crater, east of Flagstaff; Museum of Northern Arizona.

A ranger approached me, hiking up. He called out, "You must be Lora!" Female hikers I had seen earlier must have alerted him to my solo hike. He asked if I was OK. I told him I was quite thirsty and mistakenly thought that I could refill my water bottle along the way. Although there is potable water on Bright Angel Trail, there's none on the South Kaibab Trail.

The ranger offered me some of his water, convincing me that he carried extra water and wouldn't need it. He reassured me that Phantom Ranch wasn't far—and then I saw the Colorado River in the distance.

Crossing the river felt like a huge achievement. I wasn't sure how much farther Phantom Ranch was. Now I was really tired. The park service brochure estimates this hike down takes four to five hours, but for me it was nine to 10 hours.

At the ranch, I shared a cabin with nine women. Taking off my boots and socks, I saw the blisters. At dinner in the main mess hall, I sat next to a semiretired attorney celebrating her 81st birthday. Down the table, a young girl of 10 or 12 was also celebrating a birthday with her family.

The stars in the sky that night were the brightest I've ever seen. I climbed into my top bunk with cramped legs, took some Tylenol and was asleep before the cabin lights went out.

The next morning, after 4:30 a.m. breakfast, I headed out to climb the 7.8-mile Bright Angel Trail back up, my blisters covered with moleskin. When I crossed the Colorado River, knowing this was probably the last time I'd ever see it so close, I said a prayer of thanks.

The Bright Angel Trail is easier than the South Kaibab Trail, and my goal

▼
A woman hikes in Blacktail Canyon.

▼
As it soars above, this raven seems to have the best view of a Grand Canyon sunset.

Crossing the Colorado River is a milestone for hikers trekking into the canyon.

was to make it to the top before dark. I had to cross streams, and at one point I thought I'd even lost the trail. Many hikers passed me, all sharing some encouraging words.

At about 1 p.m., I realized that I wouldn't make it to the top before dark. A friend had warned me not to look up, just look back down the trail I'd traversed—good advice.

About 3 miles from the top rim, while I didn't feel any pain, I was very tired. The trail became steeper and steeper, almost like a difficult staircase to climb. I started moving more and more slowly.

At sundown I thought maybe I'll be stuck on the trail tonight, maybe I can't make it to the top. Then my grandfather's motto came to mind: I think I can, I think I can.

And then I saw a young woman, Annette, coming toward me. She said she was headed down the trail a bit to refill her water bottle, but she offered to carry my backpack for me when she returned.

Annette is the head housekeeper at Bright Angel Lodge, where she has worked for 20-plus years. I'm sure she could have hiked the final 1.5 miles up the trail in less than an hour, but she stayed with me for the next two hours, shining her flashlight ahead on the trail and chatting as we hiked. I wore my headlamp and had a flashlight, too.

I tripped once and had difficulty breathing. Annette never left my side. We finally reached the top at about 8 p.m. I know Annette's conversation and encouragement made the final ascent memorable and safe for me. So in the morning, I made a donation to the Grand Canyon Conservancy, a nonprofit organization that helps to preserve and protect the park, in Annette's name. ●

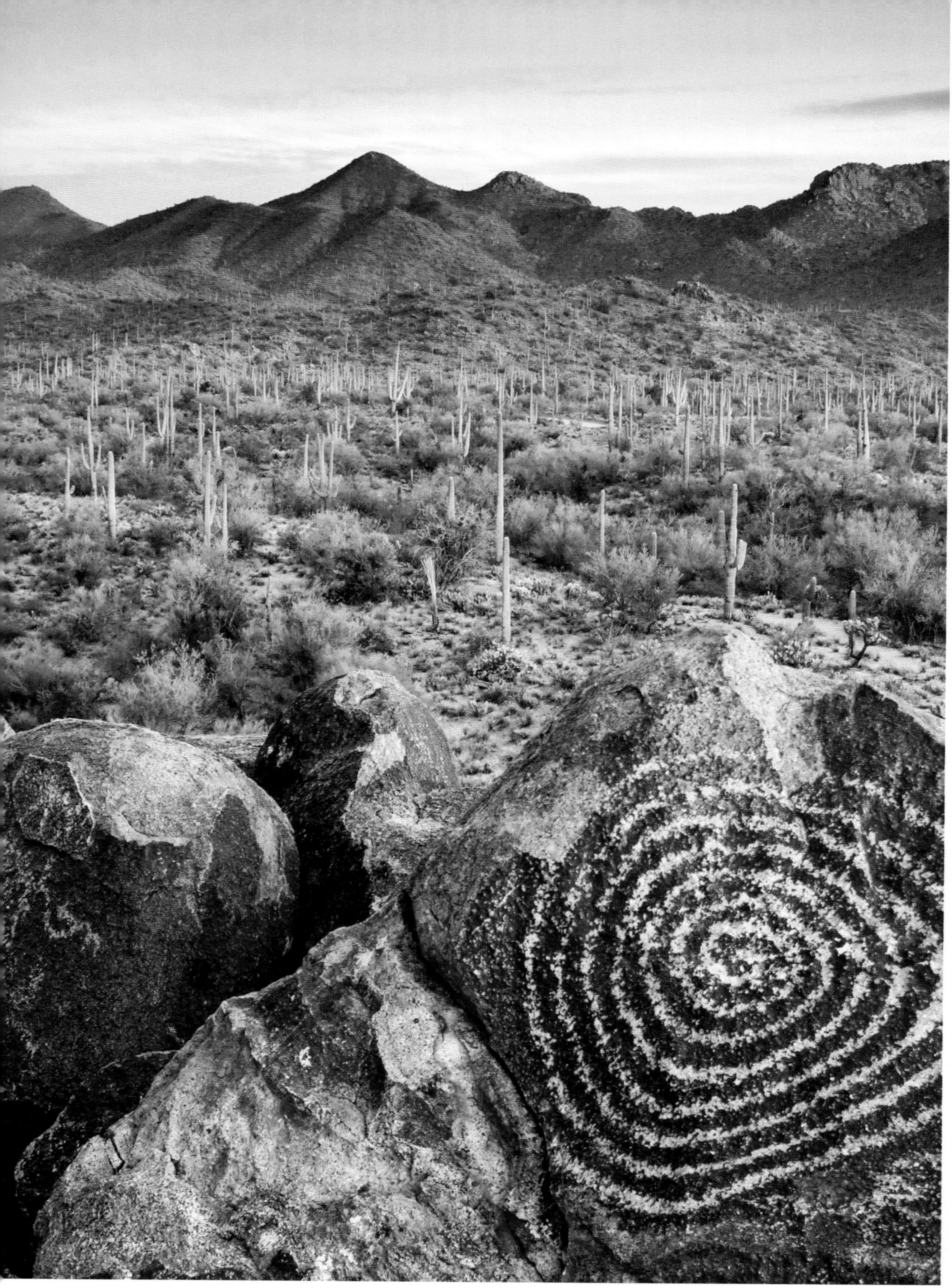

▼
Hikers often find petroglyphs along Signal Hill Trail in the park's west district.

STORY AND PHOTOS BY
RON & JANINE NIEBRUGGE

SAGUARO

AN ABUNDANCE OF CATUSES WELCOME HIKERS, CYCLISTS AND NATURE LOVERS TO THIS DESERT PARADISE.

SAGUARO CACTUSES stand out in the Sonoran Desert of Arizona. Tall with their treelike arms turned up to the sky (you could say they look like spiky green candelabras), they're an icon of the American Southwest and the star attraction at Saguaro National Park.

Let's start by learning how to pronounce this tricky word "saguaro." Remember that the "g" is silent: *sa-WAH-row*. Saguaros can live for up to 200 years, and the only place in the world where they grow is the Sonoran Desert. While growth rates may vary depending on precise location and weather, it takes about 35 years for the saguaros to produce their first signature flowers (the saguaro bloom), 50 to 100 years to grow their first arms and about 150 years to reach full height—up to 50 feet.

Split into east and west districts by the city of Tucson, Saguaro National Park preserves and protects this vital part of the desert. Though both districts feature visitor centers, picnic areas and plenty of opportunities for hiking and cycling, the terrain differs somewhat, so visiting both is a must.

With area elevations ranging from 2,180 to 8,666 feet, the plants and wildlife vary widely throughout the

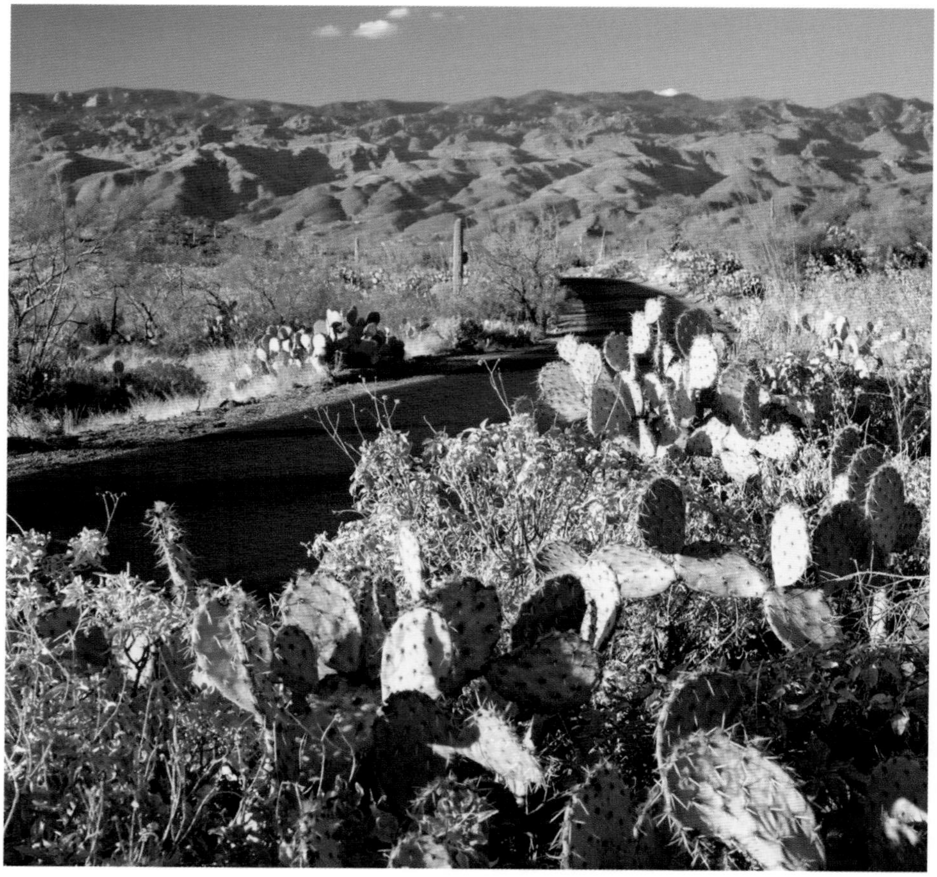

Cactus Forest Scenic Loop Drive winds past plenty of prickly pears.

POINTS OF INTEREST

FUN FACTS

The saguaros are a great boon to desert birds. Woodpeckers drill holes in the fleshy arms for nests, which are often used later by screech-owls, purple martins and sparrow hawks.

Over 50 miles of hiking and horseback-riding trails traverse a 58,000-acre wilderness and ascend to the summits of the fir-forested Rincon Mountains at an altitude of 8,700 feet.

NEARBY ATTRACTION

Though technically outside the park, the Arizona-Sonora Desert Museum will inspire you to find beauty and life in the surrounding desert.

park. Desert newcomers will find the landscape to be surprisingly lush.

The real treasure of the west district, which sits amid the Tucson Mountains, is the sheer volume of saguaros. The forest here is dense and astounding. Begin with a stop at the Red Hills Visitor Center and take in the super view from the picture window.

To truly appreciate the park, take the time to hike a trail or two (or three). Both districts have accessible trails, so there's something for everyone here. For example, the west's half-mile Desert Discovery Trail is paved and dotted with signs about the natural features of the Sonoran Desert. Valley View Overlook is another short, fairly easy trail with a stunning view of the Avra Valley and beyond. From here one can see how development has crept up to the park's boundary over the years.

The Signal Hill Trail is a must-do. It features iconic desert sunsets as well as petroglyphs etched by the Hohokam, an ancient, highly advanced Native American tribe whose disappearance in the 15th century remains something of a mystery.

If you'd rather explore the area on wheels, take the 5-mile Scenic Bajada Loop Drive by bicycle, motorbike or car. The road winds through a thick saguaro stand and has plenty of spots to pull over and take a photo.

The saguaros are not as dense in the east district. Rather, the draw here is a cactus forest, home to an abundance of desert plants including teddy bear (or jumping) cholla, barrel and prickly pear. Numerous trails on this side of the park wind through the desert terrain. Keep your eyes open for young saguaros growing under a "nurse tree" (usually a palo verde or mesquite).

Another feature of the east district is the Rincon Mountain range. These sky islands are isolated and surrounded by a lowland climate that varies radically, with forest at the top and desert at the bottom. In fact, the east district encompasses five different biomes.

The east district has its own visitor center, and we suggest starting there. Take a look at the water feature out back and see if any animals stop by for a drink. Then, drive along Cactus Forest Drive in the foothills of the Rincons. There are many trails and overlooks along this one-way loop road. Desert Ecology Trail, for example, is paved and wheelchair-accessible. For something a little longer, the Loma Verde Loop is a solid choice.

Our favorite time to visit Saguaro National Park is in the spring, from mid-March through May. The weather is perfect at this time of year and the cactuses and wildflowers bring the desert to life. In May the saguaros will bloom, producing the lovely white blossom that is Arizona's official flower.

At a minimum, allow one full day for each section of the park. Always bring water and sunscreen, even in the winter or on a cool or cloudy day. And remember to bring a comb to remove cactus spines that may attach to you.

Explore Saguaro National Park and encounter a landscape teeming with life and the spirit of the Southwest. ■

Saguaros steal the show in this Sonoran sunrise.

1.

2.

1. TRANQUILITY
On a visit to Big Bend National Park in Texas, I took a hike to the river. About half a mile along the sun started to set. I turned around and this is the awesome view I was blessed to see. – **HEATHER GROSJEAN**

2. MORNING GIFT
There was a passing storm at Grand Canyon National Park and I was trying to photograph some lightning strikes off in the distance. But, as soon as the sun broke the horizon, a double rainbow appeared instead. – **CHUCK ROBINSON**

3. ANCIENT TREES
It is fascinating that these red colored blocks of stone at the Petrified Forest National Park in Arizona were once an enormous living tree in a lush forest. The tree was nearly 3 feet in diameter. – **JOHN NUTILE**

4. LAST LIGHT
My wife and I decided to hike around Yaki Point at the Grand Canyon so we'd be ready for the sunset. This tree and the sun captured the scene as well as the heat we felt that day, which topped out at 118 degrees. – **BRAD KAVO**

3.

4.

1.

1. CASCADING WONDER
Mooney Falls is the tallest of the three waterfalls in the Havasupai Indian Reservation near Grand Canyon National Park. I thought it would be interesting to get a picture from above, showcasing both the waterfall and the majestic drop into the canyon below. I included my feet in the photo to give some perspective. – **GRANT CLOUD**

2. STRIKING
I'd been dreaming of going to the North Rim of the Grand Canyon for years, having been to the South Rim. I was hoping for beautiful clouds. The afternoon I arrived, the clouds came rolling in and to my surprise lightning flashed! – **TERRY WOOD**

3. BEACON OF HOPE
I think this image looks like a lighthouse overlooking the Grand Canyon, perhaps leading people to safety and giving them hope. (This is the Desert View Watchtower.) – **KITTA DORY**

4. BALANCED ROCK
It was amazing to see the rock formations and sit near this massive one called Balanced Rock at Big Bend National Park in Texas.
– **SARA CRENWELGE**

5. BLOOMING
The desert of Saguaro National Park comes alive after a wet winter. I drove through the park once a week during spring to see what was blooming next. Here, it's a prickly pear. – **CAROLYN OWEN**

2.

3.

4.

5.

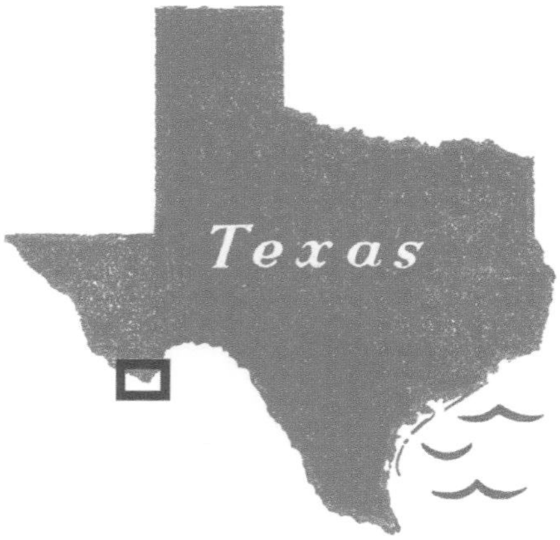

STORY BY
TIM FITZHARRIS

BIG BEND

THIS ECOLOGICAL CROSSROADS PACKS A PLETHORA OF NATURAL BEAUTY INTO A SINGLE NATIONAL PARK.

HERE IN THE 800,000-PLUS-ACRE Big Bend National Park, the Chihuahuan Desert meets the Rio Grande. The U.S. meets Mexico. Northern species meet southern ones as the boundaries of many plant and animal ranges overlap, making this remote treasure as famously diverse biologically as it is geologically.

Each year I visit this place in the great south-dipping curve of the Rio Grande, where brittle desert gives way to badlands. The land undulates with jagged rocks, flat mesas and jutting plateaus, falling and rising until finally, at its heart, soaring more than 7,000 feet skyward into the Chisos Mountains. This is my destination. By squatting low among clumps of agave and filling the frame with rising rock formations, I capture some majestic desert photos.

Everywhere, subjects appear, from the sunbaked and cactus-studded Chihuahuan Desert to the Rio Grande winding a green ribbon between dark, narrow canyons. Inside the Chisos basin, a steep waterfall fools you into forgetting that you're deep inside an arid region. Mexico's mountains dominate the southern horizon.

Each season lends a distinct flavor to the terrain. A winter dusting of snow adds zing to the desert landscape. As spring rains arrive, wildflowers and cacti burst into bloom. Springtime also means bird migration, and Big Bend hosts more bird species than any national park in the country. By late summer, visitors are treated to afternoon thunderstorms, with lightning, rainbows and rolling cloud banks embellishing an already spectacular landscape. By autumn, the fiery colors of trees and shrubs ignite mountains and bottomlands.

Yes, deciduous trees grow alongside the southwestern pinyon pine and juniper, which—like many other northern and southern, eastern and western species—meet in this central region. Straddling subclimates, Big Bend might be the foremost place to experience the best of North, Central and South America combined. ■

Top: Looking out on an expansive view in the basin at Big Bend. Bottom: Black-tailed jack rabbits nibbling grass often venture close to campsites.

POINTS OF INTEREST

NOT TO BE MISSED

A must-see if you are up for a hike is the Lost Mine Trail.

Best views can be had at Santa Elena Canyon and the Chisos Mountains.

FUN FACTS

Big Bend Country is named for the great curve of the Rio Grande where it rounds the southern elbow of Texas.

The diverse habitats support 1,200 types of plants, around 450 bird species and varied wildlife, including mountain lions and javelinas.

WORDS TO THE WISE

You can't see everything in one day, but take the paved Ross Maxwell Scenic Drive for a sampling of what the park has to offer. Dirt roads crisscross the park, and gravel roads are open to horse riders.

When hiking, wear cool, rugged clothing for protection from prickly plants and take along at least 1 gallon of water per person per day.

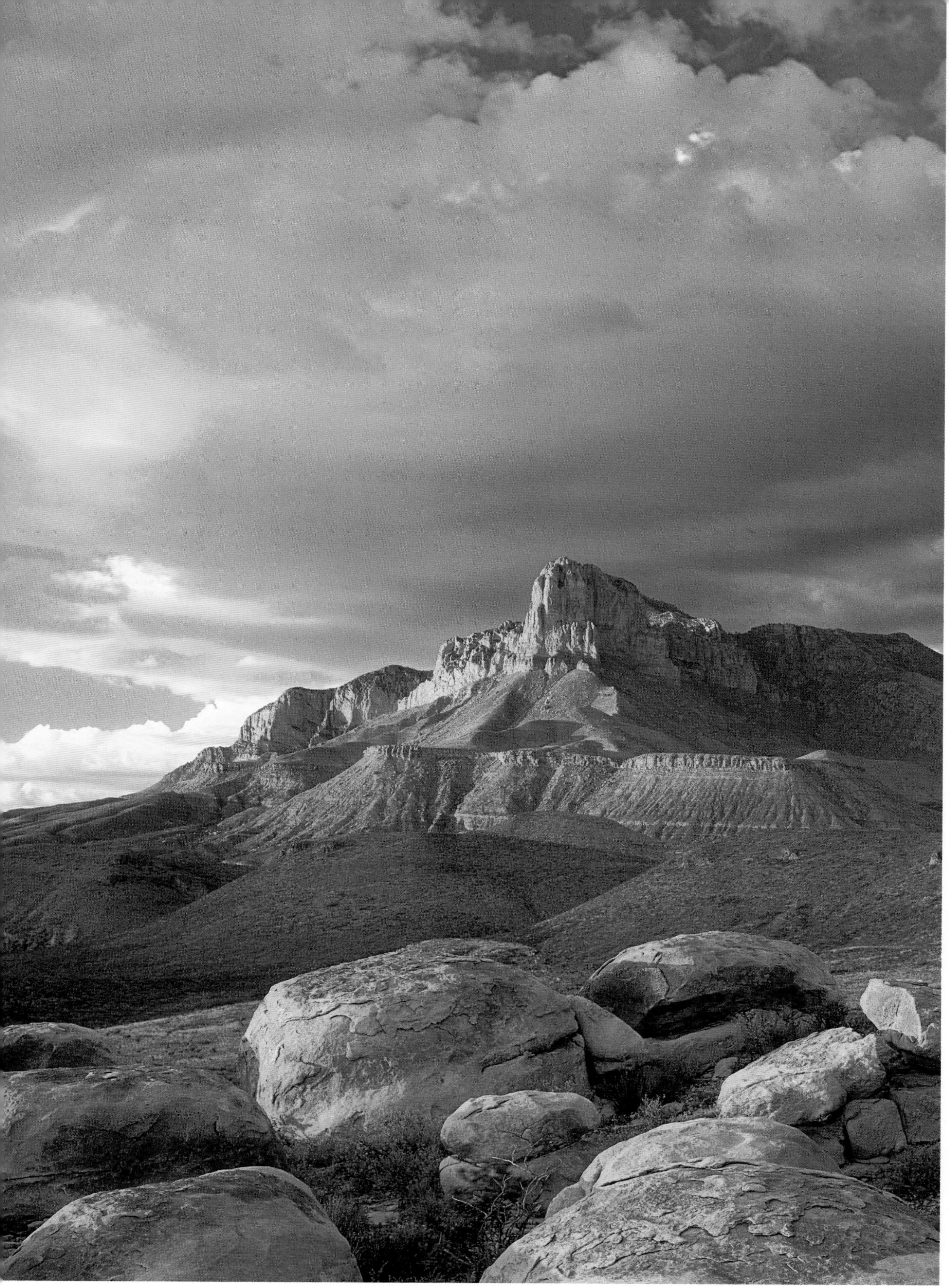

▼
Years of wind and rain have eroded the massive limestone face of El Capitan.

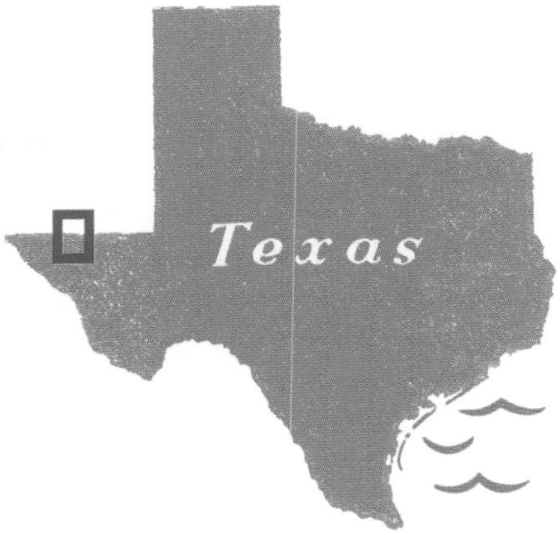

STORY AND PHOTOS BY
LAURENCE PARENT

GUADALUPE MOUNTAINS

UNCOVERING THE SECRETS OF THIS REMOTE RANGE REQUIRES STURDY BOOTS AND A LITTLE SWEAT.

AS I DRIVE ACROSS the creosote-dotted plains northwest of Pecos, Texas, I get my first glimpse of Guadalupe Mountains National Park. Slowly, the mountains seem to grow taller as I approach, the hazy outline resolving into a rugged line of craggy peaks. The temperature drops as the desert scrub is replaced by the grasses and the widely scattered junipers of the foothills.

By the time I pull into the visitor center parking lot, the peaks tower almost 3,000 feet above me. The steep slopes and cliffs look quite harsh and unforgiving, although a few scattered pines, junipers and even red blotches of maples tucked into ravines high above give a small hint of what lies hidden here.

Guadalupe Mountains National Park is an isolated place with 86 miles of trails and three different ecosystems. The nearest town is 55 miles away, and gorgeous scenery abounds. The only thing missing is the crowds.

I set up my tent in the park campground and drive over to the historic Frijole Ranch house, where early settlers built their home at a spring that they used to water a fruit orchard and a vegetable garden. After studying the exhibits in the restored house, I begin the easy loop hike to Smith Spring. I quickly reach Manzanita Spring, where clear water fills a cattail-lined pond.

From Manzanita Spring, I follow the trail toward a canyon, where the mountains begin their abrupt rise into the high country above. I walk into a grove of ponderosa pines, alligator junipers and other trees. Thick trees harbor the hidden waters of Smith Spring. Bigtooth maple trees, their

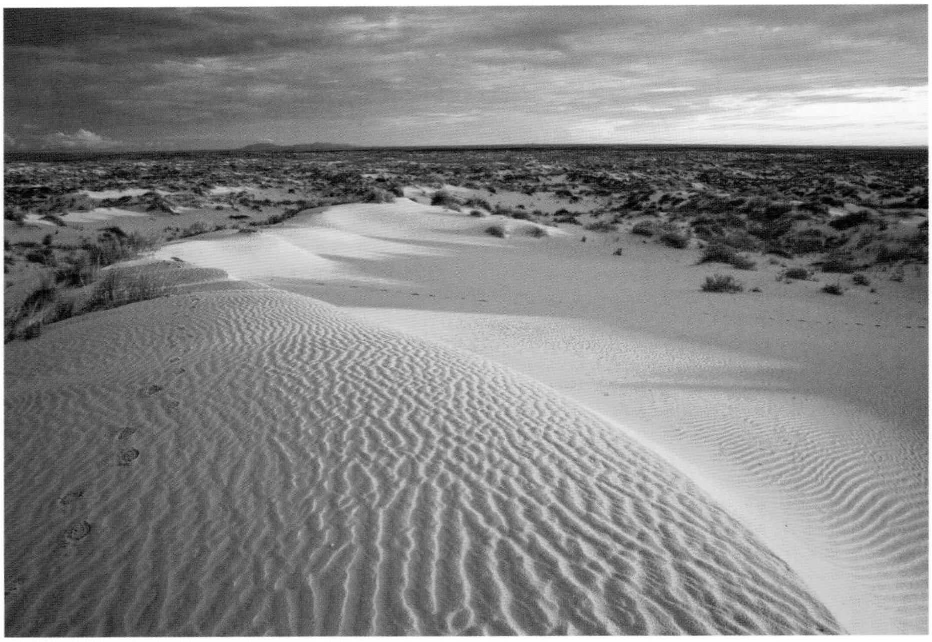

The last light of day illuminates ripples in the sand dunes.

POINTS OF INTEREST

NOT TO BE MISSED
Guadalupe Peak is also known as the "Top of Texas." A hike up the side is tough, but definitely rewarding. It's about an 8.5-mile round trip that may take you 6 to 8 hours. You'll encounter different ecosystems along the way, including high desert and high elevation forests.

WORDS TO THE WISE
The rough dirt road leading to Williams Ranch is the one place in the park where mountain biking is permitted.

NEARBY ATTRACTIONS
Hueco Tanks State Park and Historic Site; McDonald Observatory; Fort Davis National Historic Site

leaves aflame with gold, orange and scarlet, arch over the small stream that trickles through the woods.

The next morning I rise early and drive to the McKittrick Canyon trailhead. Although many call the canyon the "most beautiful spot in Texas," you might miss it because the canyon walls are mostly covered with hardy desert vegetation. The easy trail follows the canyon bottom upstream.

I crisscross the dry canyon bottom, its surface covered with rounded limestone cobbles. A few junipers and oaks appear as I move deeper into the canyon. At about 2 miles I pause at the stone house built by Wallace Pratt, the petroleum geologist who donated much of the canyon to the National Park Service. From there I walk up into South McKittrick Canyon, admiring the maple trees that grow thickly with other trees in the lush canyon bottom and dot the steep slopes above with bright colors. At the trail's end I relax in the shade and listen to a tumbling stream as the breeze blows colorful leaves off the maples. I now understand the canyon's reputation.

For my last day, I awake early and begin the long climb up the 8,749-foot Guadalupe Peak, the highest point in Texas. The steep yet excellent trail soon has me sweating and breathing hard. Three thousand vertical feet and 4.2 miles later, I collapse onto the craggy summit. Sheer cliffs line the west edge of the peak, dropping 5,000 vertical feet to the desolate Salt Flats below. West Texas and southern New Mexico sprawl out in every direction.

Looking at the horizon, I see limestone cliffs all around me. The white stone was created 250 million years ago when these mountains were a reef in a vast, ancient sea. To the north lies the mountain high country, a relict forest of ponderosa pine, Douglas fir, white pine and even a few aspens. None of this is visible from below. At Guadalupe Mountains National Park, I have to work to discover its secrets. ■

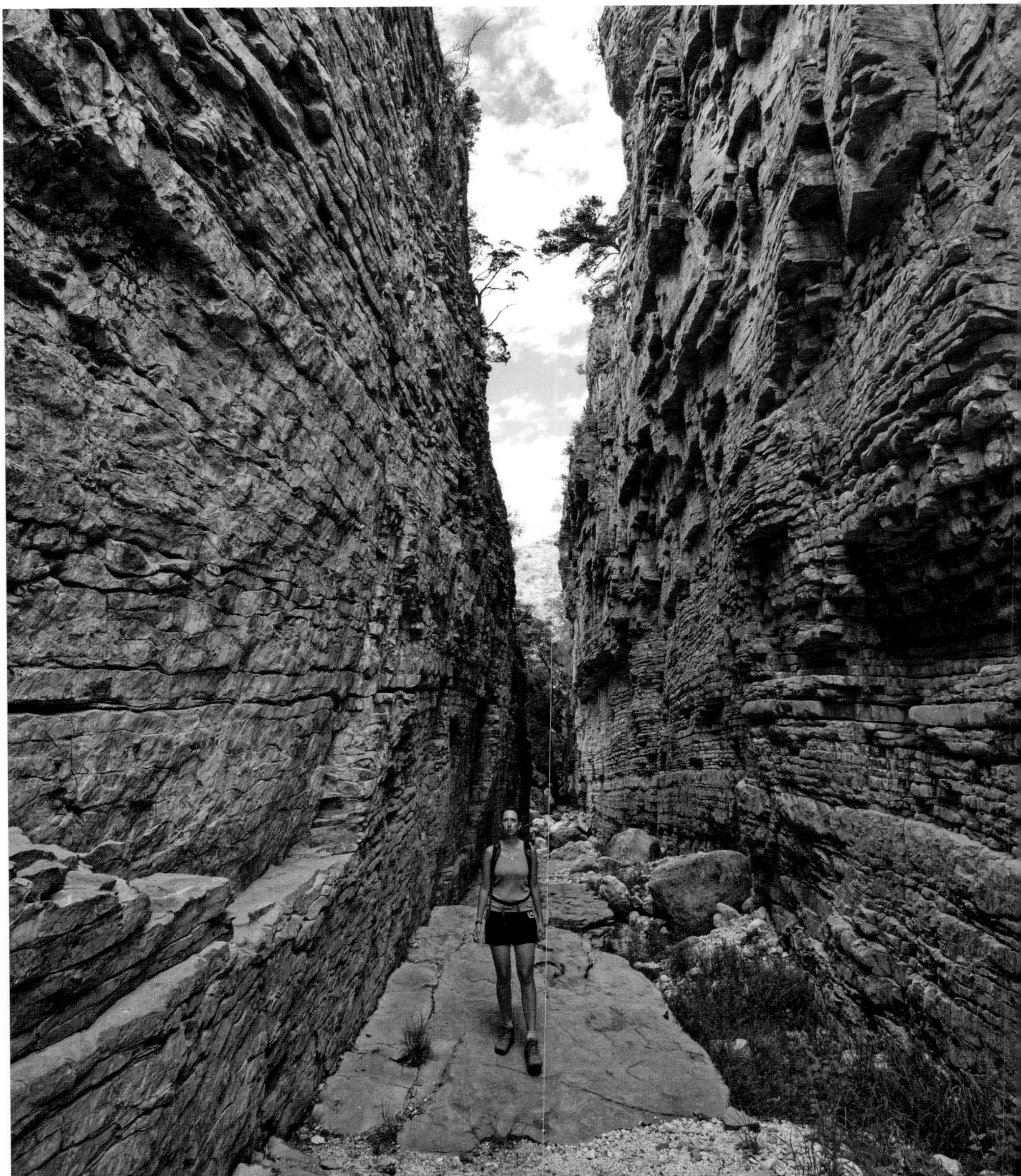

▼
Hiker Heather Dobbins explores a slot canyon.

GRAND CANYON NATIONAL PARK

1930s

The view from the steep cliff at Toroweap Overlook on the North Rim of the Grand Canyon is timeless, as seen in this vintage photo.

2015

Not much has changed with the spectacular scene overlooking the Colorado River, 3,000 feet below. It is still difficult to access, but visitors in both these photos know exactly what to do when they get there: take it all in at just the right spot.

THEN: EIVIND T. SCOYEN/ U.S. NATIONAL PARK SERVICE; NOW: PIRIYA PHOTOGRAPHY/ GETTY IMAGES

MIDWEST
DUNES · LAKESHORES · PRAIRIES

RUSSELL KORD/ALAMY STOCK PHOTO

▼
The sand dune Mount Baldy stands 120 feet above the beach.

STORY BY
MARSHA WILLIAMSON MOHR

INDIANA DUNES

CLEAR WATER, SANDY BEACHES AND ABUNDANT WILDLIFE CREATE AN OASIS ON THE SOUTHERN TIP OF LAKE MICHIGAN.

THE WEEKEND AFTER Labor Day, my husband, Larry, and I go to Indiana Dunes National Park to camp with friends. We set up tents about 4 miles from our favorite beach, so bringing bikes is a must.

With a day's supply of towels, coolers and toys, we pedal hard to the shore. Larry takes floating noodles, and one friend packs a bubble maker on their bike. It's a truly idyllic way to see and experience Indiana Dunes.

The park is an oasis with 15 miles of beaches surrounded by tall sand grass, and a lakeshore that is one of the most biologically diverse sites in the national park system. It has about 15,000 acres of natural terrain, with marshland and jack pine forest, hundreds of flower species, and many animals such as egrets, white-tailed deer, great blue herons and red fox, to name a few.

The Indiana Dunes lakeshore area is so beloved that it became a national park in 2019, as the latest step in an ongoing effort to save these pristine dunes that began in 1899, when industry and preservationists battled to control this shore. In 1966, the ecosystem won when the area was declared a national lakeshore.

Today, visitors climb to the top of the big sand dunes and then run back to the bottom. It's a tradition loved by children most of all. The clear waters invite a swim—one of my favorite things to do, especially at sunset.

Larry and I have hiked most of the 50 miles of trails. We love seeing the array of plant and animal life. Tamarack trees, floating mats of sphagnum moss, and blueberry bushes grow along the Pinhook Bog Trail System. Rare flowers like pink lady's slippers and yellow orchids

Visitors can hike up and down the dunes on boardwalk steps.

dazzle hikers. (Sandy conditions on the trails require a bit more exertion, so bring plenty of water.)

The 4.7-mile Cowles Bog Trail winds through a pristine beach habitat, an 8,000-year-old fen (open wetland), a lowland forest of red maple, and a yellow birch and black oak savanna. This part of the park is named for Henry Cowles, whose plant studies led to its designation as a National Natural Landmark.

Birders flock to the Great Marsh Trail to spot coots, sandhill cranes and wood ducks. During migration, warblers, kingfishers, tree swallows and rusty blackbirds come to rest. Animal activity is a huge draw along the Great Marsh.

On our way back to camp we have to stop at a local gas station for soft-serve ice cream. It's the perfect, refreshing end to a day of exploration in one of Indiana's natural treasures. ■

POINTS OF INTEREST

FUN FACT
Indiana Dunes National Park has 352 species of birds—even more than Great Smoky Mountains National Park, which has 240.

WORDS TO THE WISE
Because of the hidden dangers of shifting sands that could be covered by snow in winter, sledding, inner-tubing, tobogganing, skiing and snowboarding are prohibited in the park.

NOT TO BE MISSED
You can experience Indiana Dunes by train! This park is part of a parternship the National Park Service has with Amtrak and the Texas A&M Department of Recreation, Park & Tourism Sciences. Passengers can experience the beauty of nature in a completely unique way, as volunteers lead the tour aboard the train and explain why certain sites along the route are meaningful.

▼ *Indiana Dunes National Park offers stunning views of Lake Michigan*

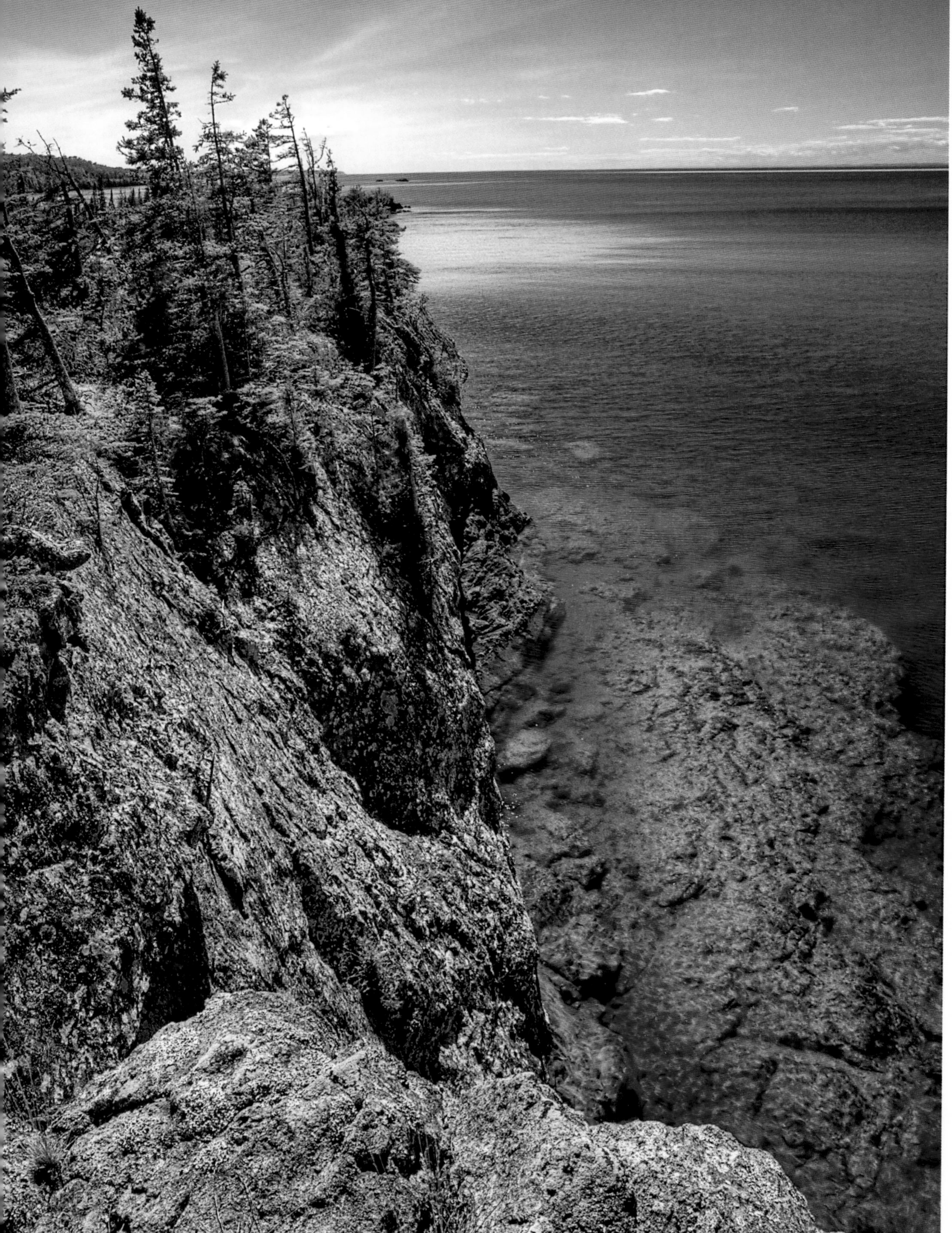

▼
Kamloops Point was named for a ship that sank a couple of hundred yards away in 1927.

STORY AND PHOTOS BY
CARL TERHAAR

ISLE ROYALE

FEW VENTURE OUT TO THESE ISOLATED ISLANDS, BUT THOSE WHO DO CAN'T WAIT TO RETURN.

SURROUNDED BY WATER, this unsung national park is truly a hidden gem. Those who make the trip to Isle Royale are drawn to the beauty of 337 miles of shoreline along Lake Superior and the peacefulness of one of the country's more isolated areas east of the Mississippi River.

Fewer visitors does not mean that Isle Royale and the 400 islands in its archipelago aren't beautiful or delightful. It only means this park is a little harder to get to than most. You can't drive there, and you'll find no roads after you arrive.

And once visitors fall for the park's unspoiled serenity, many come back time and time again. It's not unusual to hear conversations on the ferry boats about who can boast the most trips to the island.

After you disembark, the only way to travel through the archipelago is along hiking trails or waterways—on foot and in small boats—just as French fur trappers, known as voyageurs, explored the area hundreds of years ago.

Positioned about 15 miles off the shore of Canada, the 45-mile-long island is the largest in the "Big Lake." Setting off from Michigan or Minnesota adds a boat or seaplane ride to the adventure. Isle Royale National Park is served by ferries that depart from Grand Portage in Minnesota or Copper Harbor and Houghton in Michigan, and

The waters of Tobin Harbor catch the sunrise.

POINTS OF INTEREST

FUN FACTS

More than 600 flowering plants grow at Isle Royale National Park, including over 40 endangered or threatened species.

During the exceptionally cold winter of 1948-49, an ice bridge formed between Canada and Isle Royale, and a small pack of Eastern timber wolves crossed over to the island. Offshoots of the original pack became established there at one point. The wolves are important to maintaining a healthy moose population on the island by preying on the very old, sick or injured.

WORDS TO THE WISE

No pets are allowed on the island.

also by seaplane from the Houghton County airport.

This remoteness is one reason the average length of stay at Isle Royale is four days. After going through the effort to get there, you will definitely want to stay awhile to bask in the surroundings and the solitude.

Lake Superior not only contributes to the mystique and the sublime scenery with its rocky shorelines; it also has a major influence on the weather. Slow to warm up in the spring, it can cause a great deal of fog, especially in early summer. The water keeps the air cooler near the shore, while air in the higher ridges away from the lake can often be 20 degrees warmer.

The clear lake water provides excellent visibility for fishing for fresh trout or scuba diving to explore Lake Superior's many shipwrecks.

The size of the lake has also affected animal life on the island. Only half of the species on the mainland have been able to cross over. There are no bears, skunks or raccoons, and only two snake species.

With fewer ice bridges forming to the mainland in the last few decades, the possibility of new blood making its way to Isle Royale is slim.

Animal lovers who visit the island hoping to see wolves and moose might be rewarded with moose sightings. That population has increased. The wolf population has declined through the years. The National Park Service, however, is carefully reintroducing new wolves to sustain the ecosystem.

Many come to backpack the 165 miles of marked trails. Scattered throughout the park and along its inland lakes are 36 designated campgrounds, accessible by foot, canoe or kayak.

Kayakers and canoers also venture out onto Superior; some sites on Superior's shore have docks for sailboats or motorboats. Each year, a handful of expert paddlers take a week or two to circumnavigate the island, with a few extra days allotted in case of bad weather.

But most kayakers take shorter trips and stick to the more protected harbors in the island's long, narrow bays. The *Voyageur II* out of Grand Portage and a water taxi operated by the Rock Harbor Lodge can ferry you and your canoe or kayak to and from the campgrounds, trailheads and docks along their circuits around the island.

If you are looking for comfort and a soft bed, you can find them at Rock Harbor Lodge on the east end of the island. Rent a room, cottage or cabin. The lodge also operates a restaurant, stores that offer groceries and camping supplies, and a marina with gasoline and diesel fuel.

Rock Harbor is where you can get camping permits and rent canoes or small outboard boats to go exploring on your own. Guided tours on the MV *Sandy* offer a chance to see the historic Edisen Fishery and the Rock Harbor Lighthouse, the oldest on the island. Other cruises head off to Lookout Louise, with views of Ontario and Isle Royale's north side, or to Raspberry Island at sunset. You also can charter a fishing trip to catch salmon and trout.

Surrounded by the world's largest lake, feel the enormity of the universe and dance with the Northern Lights while you plan your return trip to the glorious Isle Royale. ■

As Lake Superior's water level rises, daisies on Johnson Island get their feet wet.

STORY BY **MARY LIZ AUSTIN**
PHOTOS BY **TERRY DONNELLY**

PICTURED ROCKS

MOTHER NATURE BLENDED HER MOST BREATHTAKING COLORS AND TEXTURES TO CREATE THIS NORTHERN MASTERPIECE.

PICTURED ROCKS NATIONAL LAKESHORE on Michigan's Upper Peninsula is one of our favorite autumn destinations. The northern forest's brilliantly colored leaves combine with the clear blue waters of Lake Superior to paint some spectacular fall scenes.

But when we stop for supplies, my husband and I can't help overhearing excited chatter about an impending snowstorm. The Yoopers, as locals are known, eagerly anticipate the prospect of early skiing, but Terry and I hope the snow won't end up burying our entire photography season.

The lakeshore is named for 200-foot bluffs colored by mineral-rich water seeping through layers of sandstone that have been sculpted into dramatic columns and caves by winds, waves and ice. With a backdrop of Superior's blue waters and autumn leaves, it's quite a show. The trail to Miner's Castle, the most famous formation, offers incredible views of the shoreline and lake.

But that's just the beginning. Two quaint towns anchor either end of the national lakeshore. On the western end, Munising boasts Munising Falls, a 50-foot ponytail waterfall in a beautiful sheltered canyon of yellow sandstone. On the eastern end, the town of Grand Marais offers easy access to Au Sable Point Lighthouse, Grand Sable Dunes and Sable Falls. And rolling, winding County Road H-58, which connects the two towns, ranks among the most scenic drives in America.

The overnight storm brings only a dusting of snow, so we get out early to see if we can capture some sunrise light, and it is cold. I'm shivering in my winter parka and every bit of wool I own when I notice several Yoopers hiking by. They're easily recognizable by the light nylon jackets they wear, as if it's a warm fall day. You have to be a hardy soul to live up here, but I guess that's part of what helps preserve the unspoiled beauty of this very special place. ■

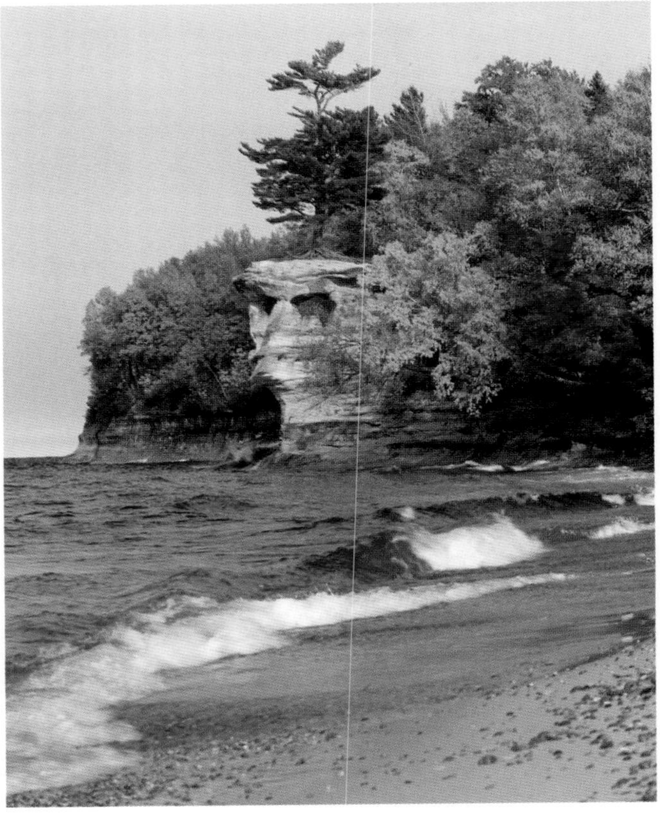

Top: A gorgeous sunset decorates Miners Beach. Bottom: Chapel Rock, embraced by fall foliage.

FUN FACTS

The cliffs at Pictured Rocks draw many visitors, but they're not the only habitat worth exploring in the park. Inland lakes, bogs, marshes and pools are great places to see some of Pictured Rocks' 60 identified species of fish and amphibians.

Painted Rocks' Au Sable light station was built in 1874 as a way to keep boats afloat—and away from the jagged coast—during inclement weather. Originally called "Big Sable," the name was changed in 1910 to better reflect its proximity to Lake Superior; "Au Sable" means "of the sand" in French.

SIDE TRIP

A trip to upper Michigan wouldn't be complete without taking a trip to the Tahquamenon Falls State Park, a notable destination for both Michigan residents and tourists.

▼

Sunny beaches littered with Petoskey stones invite travelers to stop and relax.

STORY AND PHOTOS BY
DARRYL BEERS

SLEEPING BEAR DUNES

THE WORLD'S LARGEST FRESHWATER DUNE SYSTEM SETS THE STAGE FOR THE CHARMING TOWNS AND STUNNING SCENERY ON MICHIGAN'S WEST COAST.

I WAS ABOUT 10 YEARS OLD when I joined my peers for a day of frolicking in the waves at an expansive beach on lower Michigan's western shore. I don't remember exactly where that beach was, but I vividly recall how much fun we had. I've been visiting that splendid shore as often as I can ever since.

The coastline's signature attraction is known as the singing sands, for the squeaky sound you'll hear as you walk across them. Visitors and locals alike delight in endless miles of swimming, beaches and over 300,000 acres of dunes—the largest freshwater dune system on the planet.

The most prominent of these dunes is found in Sleeping Bear Dunes National Lakeshore, on the northern tier of lower Michigan. The dunes there tower as high as 400 feet and are ideal for hiking, biking, climbing or sightseeing. Sleeping Bear Dunes is also home to lush forests, clear inland lakes and unique flora and fauna, all of which combine to make it the most beautiful place in all of America.

Do you doubt the authority of such a statement? Well, consider this: In 2011, Sleeping Bear Dunes won that exact title in a vote by almost 100,000 viewers of ABC's *Good Morning America.*

My favorite city on Michigan's western shore is Ludington, because it's fun to get there—via a four-hour cruise aboard a refurbished car ferry, SS *Badger,* which first set sail in 1953. From mid-May through late October, the ship carries passengers and vehicles between Ludington and Wisconsin. The focus for recreation in Ludington is Stearns Park Beach, which offers 2,500 feet of sandy shore.

My favorite drive in the area is Highway M-116 north out of Ludington. Though only about 6 miles long, the road hugs the shoreline with its sand beach on one side and stretches of dunes on the other.

The road ends at Ludington State Park, which by most accounts is Michigan's most popular. I've spent countless hours combing the beaches here and hiking to the historic Big

POINTS OF INTEREST

FUN FACT

The name "Sleeping Bear" comes from a Native American story about the largest dune in the park, called Mother Bear; at that time, the dune looked like a bear at rest.

WORDS TO THE WISE

Bring a pair of shoes if you plan to hike on the dunes. While the sand might feel nice on your bare feet at first, the National Park Service warns the sand can be hot and abrasive.

NEARBY ATTRACTIONS

Cruise down the 7-mile Pierce Stocking Drive to soak up the scenery, especially at the Lake Michigan Overlook. At nearly 450 feet above the lake, the overlook offers breathtaking views of the Sleeping Bear dunes far away in the distance. And, for those who aren't keen on a long walk, the overlook is just a short hike from the parking lot.

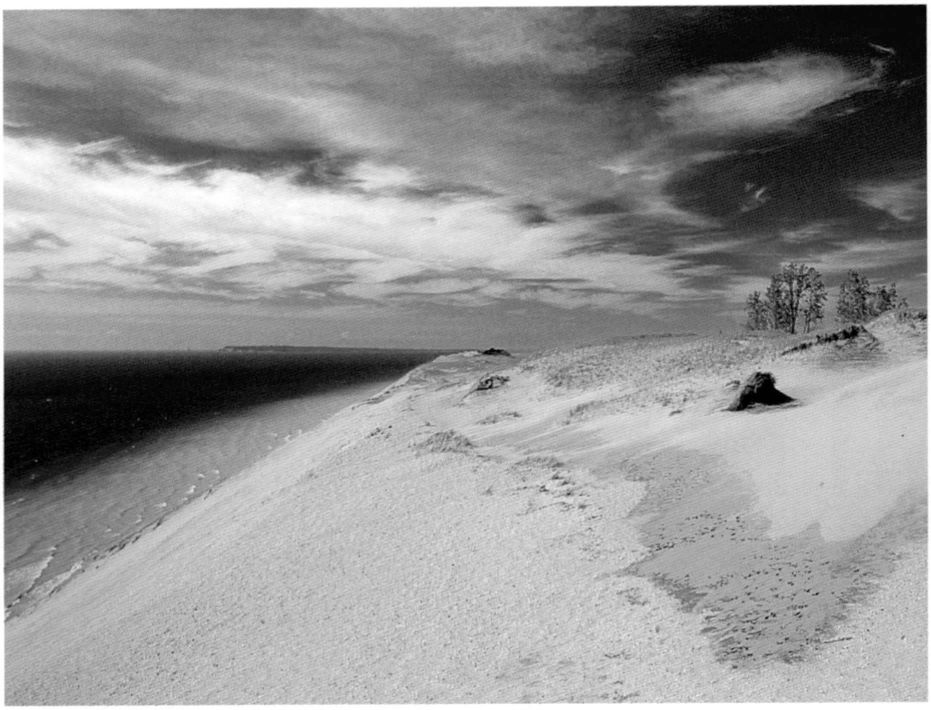

Lake Michigan meets Sleeping Bear Dunes National Lakeshore.

Sable Point Lighthouse. At 112 feet, this light is one of the tallest in Michigan. From May through October, it's open to the public for the strenuous, but rewarding, climb to the top.

But there's much more to lower Michigan's west coast than singing sands and sparkling water. The city of Holland hosts its Tulip Time Festival each May, when millions of brilliant beauties bloom at once. I fondly recall childhood trips here, where I was dazzled by the display of colors and patterns in both the tulips and the Dutch costumes of the performers.

Two additional nods to Holland's heritage are Nelis' Dutch Village, which re-creates the Netherlands of the 1800s with 10 acres of authentic architecture, canals and gardens, and the city's DeZwaan Windmill. Built in the Netherlands in 1761, the remarkable historic mill was dismantled, then shipped here in pieces and carefully reassembled in 1964. It's the only authentic working Dutch windmill in the U.S. And it's still grinding flour, which is sold to tourists, bakers and numerous restaurateurs.

Not far from the site of all this Dutch influence, Michigan's west coast also boasts more than its share of elegant Victorian architecture. In the later 1800s, steamships brought a huge influx of visitors from Chicago. Seeking a summer refuge on this breezy shore, many built ornate second homes here. Scores of these 19th century houses survive, and many have been converted into cozy bed-and-breakfasts.

A bit to the south, many Chicago painters and sculptors were drawn to the communities of Saugatuck and Douglas. The art colony continues to thrive, with so many galleries and outdoor sculptures on display that the area proudly calls itself Michigan's "art coast."

During my first visit to these twin cities, I was fascinated to witness the *Saugatuck Chain Ferry* in action. Built in 1838 to haul horses across the Kalamazoo River, the boat—said to be the only hand-cranked ferry still running in the U.S.—is now a tourist attraction, carrying passengers and bicycles. The ferry is still run by a crank attached to a chain along the river bottom; it takes about 200 cranks and five minutes to cross the 100-yard-wide river.

Farther to the north, Traverse City, which is nestled at the base of Grand Traverse Bay, lays claim to being the world's cherry capital. Its weeklong National Cherry Festival, held every July, draws a crowd of about 500,000 with everything from pie to parades.

The city is also home to three tall ships: the schooners *Manitou* and *Madeline,* and the sloop *Welcome.* Through educational and recreational programs, these three working replicas of 19th century vessels submerge visitors in maritime history.

My favorite scenic drive here follows Highway M-37 north from Traverse City through Old Mission Peninsula, which last year made *USA Today's* list of the nation's most scenic coastal routes. The trip is especially grand in the spring, when both sides of the roadway are awash in a sea of beautiful cherry blossoms.

The same climate that makes cherry trees thrive here is also a good one for European grapes, so vineyards abound along the route. The 18-mile drive through the peninsula ends at Mission Point Lighthouse, a magnificent place to photograph.

Northeast of the peninsula, not far from the tip of lower Michigan, is the

Historic DeZwaan Windmill is part of Holland's Dutch heritage.

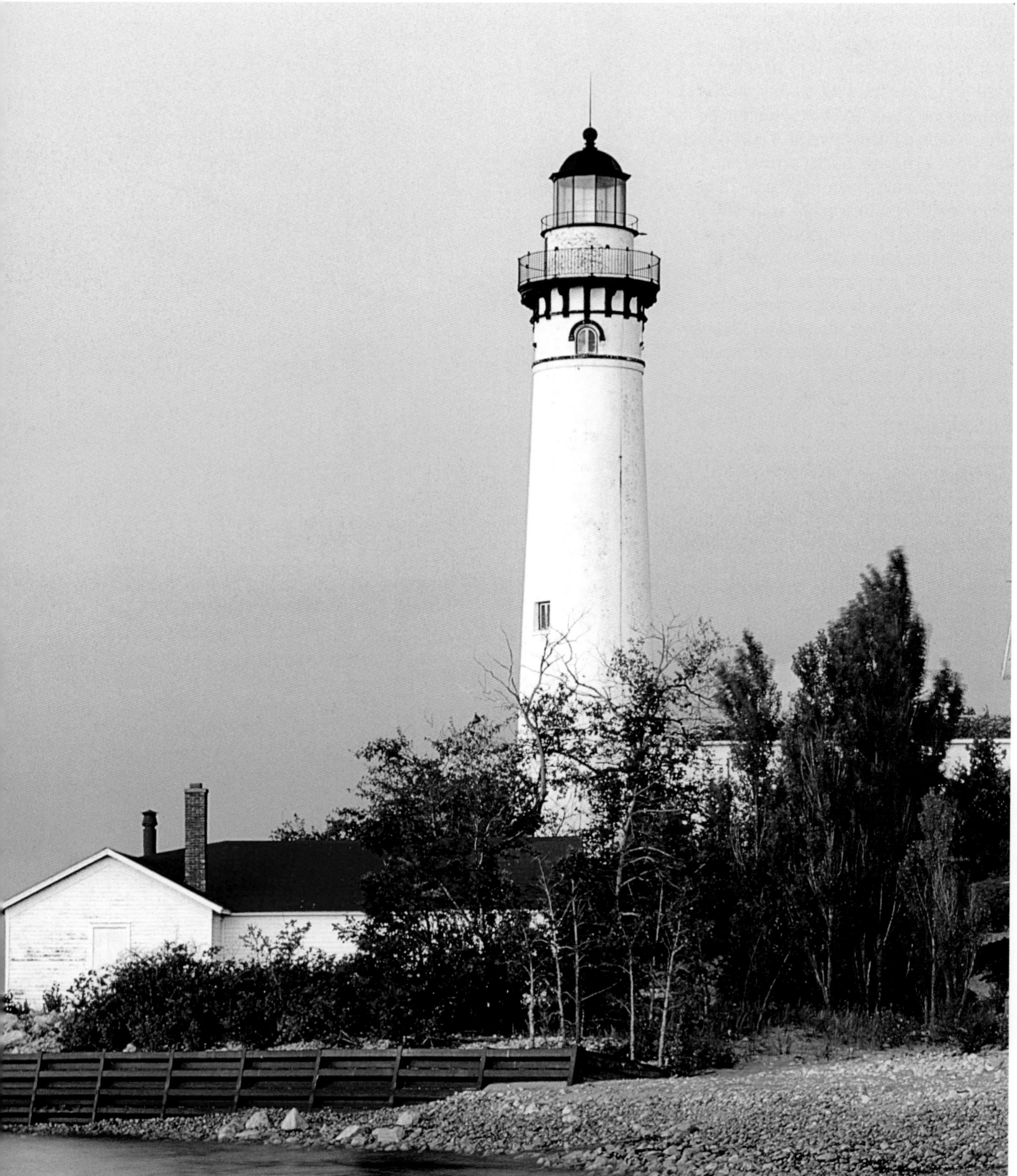

▼
The South Manitou Island Lighthouse is a tricky climb, but the views are worth the effort.

Michigan's Leelanau Peninsula boasts brilliant cherry blossoms.

fisherman's paradise of Walloon Lake, where the young Ernest Hemingway spent many summers at his family's cottage. Devoted readers can follow in the writer's footsteps on a self-guided "Hemingway tour" of the area.

Accolades for Michigan's west coast would be incomplete without bringing up three islands off the northern shore. North and South Manitou islands are part of the Sleeping Bear lakeshore and are accessible by ferry service from Leland, a historic fishing community. They have no permanent residents, and no vehicles are allowed—but hiking, backpacking, picnicking and rustic camping are permitted.

I cherish the memory of the two peaceful nights I spent camping on South Manitou. I was planning to get to bed early so I could photograph the island's lighthouse at dawn, but I was utterly unable to resist one of the most incredible nights of stargazing one could imagine. A good night's sleep had to wait.

Then there's the very different but also inviting Beaver Island, Lake Michigan's largest island, with a cozy year-round population of about 650 that swells to some 3,500 on summer weekends. A ferry running out of Charlevoix takes people and cars to and from the island. The isle has a history of Mormon settlement and an influx of Irish fishermen.

There are many great attractions at Sleeping Bear, but it's those beautiful beaches that keep luring me back to this special part of Michigan. I have no doubt that anyone who, on a warm summer evening, strolls barefoot on the sand and basks in the glowing light of a Lake Michigan sunset will realize they're standing in God's Country.

1.

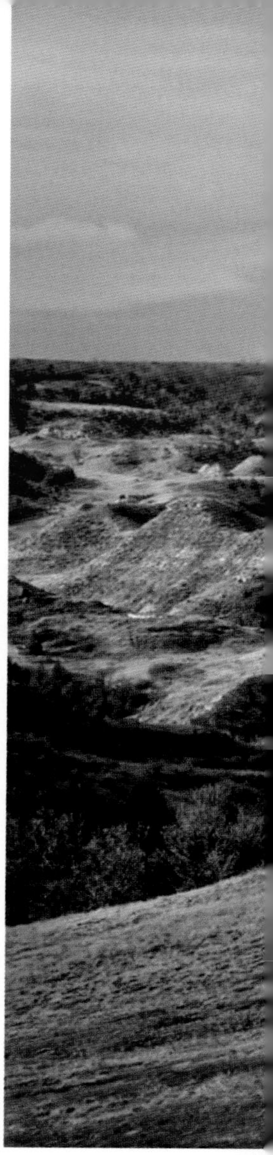
2.

1. SPECTACULAR SUNSETS
One of our favorite parks in northern Michigan is Sleeping Bear Dunes National Lakeshore. From stop 9, you can look over Lake Michigan—and you might be able to spot one of the many Great Lakes freighters. – **JERRY STUTZMAN**

2. NEVER THE SAME TWICE
Theodore Roosevelt National Park is in my home state. I try to go there at least once a year, and sometimes I am lucky enough to go there more often. – **KATHERINE PLESSNER**

3. PEACEFUL GRAZING
I saw this pronghorn in Theodore Roosevelt National Park. They're the fastest land animal in North America, but this one paused for a moment on the grass. – **LISA DOUGLASS**

4. MICHIGAN'S GLORY
This is one of my favorite views in Sleeping Bear Dunes. Lake Michigan in all her glory—with colors that rival the Caribbean—along with the dunes and perfect blue sky make this the epitome of a Michigan summer "up north." – **RENEE TOWNSEND**

3.

4.

1.

2.

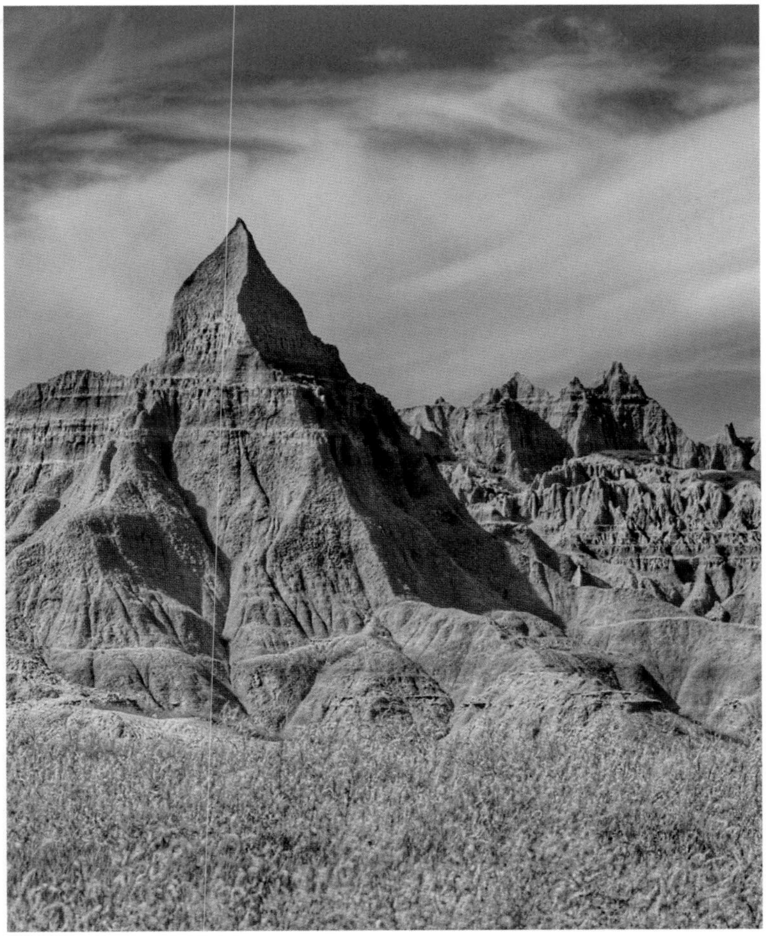
3.

4.

1. BEYOND BEAUTIFUL
Pictured Rocks has gorgeous cliffs with a beautiful forest. You can go hiking, kayaking, snowshoeing and cross-country skiing. –**DIANE CUNNINGHAM**

2. DON'T MISS IT
We visited Theodore Roosevelt National Park in July. Someone told us to go to the Painted Canyon to see the sunset. Wow—so beautiful! –**KIRSTEN BUSSE**

3. UNEXPECTED COLOR
I always envisioned the Badlands to be a vast monochromatic terrain—a dry and dim scene. Boy, was I ever wrong! We discovered sunbathing bison, bluebird skies, and lush greenery hugging the base of these incredible rock formations. –**AMY MUIR**

4. SUPER CUTE
This photo of a prairie dog was taken in Badlands National Park. Trying to catch this picture was quite a feat! They appear cuddly, but I know they have quite the temper. –**MARY HENDERSON**

1.

1. STARRY-EYED
This is a self-portrait taken on the beaches of the Sleeping Bear Dunes in Michigan. After I hit the shutter to start this 25-second exposure, I ran into the frame, froze in place and pointed my flash light to the core of the Milky Way. – **JOHN BERRY**

2. PRETTY COLORS
I snapped this photo on an evening cruise of the Apostle Islands National Lakeshore. I loved how the late-day sun made the rocks light up with a soft, warm glow. – **ADAM SMITH**

3. WHAT ON EARTH?
Where am I? Am I walking on the moon? I didn't know what to expect as to the lay of the land at Badlands National Park, but I was certainly surprised. – **WALT MATHER**

4. UNTAMED BEAUTY
During this difficult season of COVID-19, Theodore Roosevelt National Park was empty and the wild horses abounded. – **SABINA ROBBINS**

5. RETURN TRIP
Pictured Rocks National Lakeshore is relatively close to me, yet I hadn't visited for decades. So last fall my wife and I spent a week re-exploring the area. Even though the upper observation deck was crowded, I waited for my opportunity to set up and capture this image. – **DAVID HEILMAN**

2.

3.

4.

5.

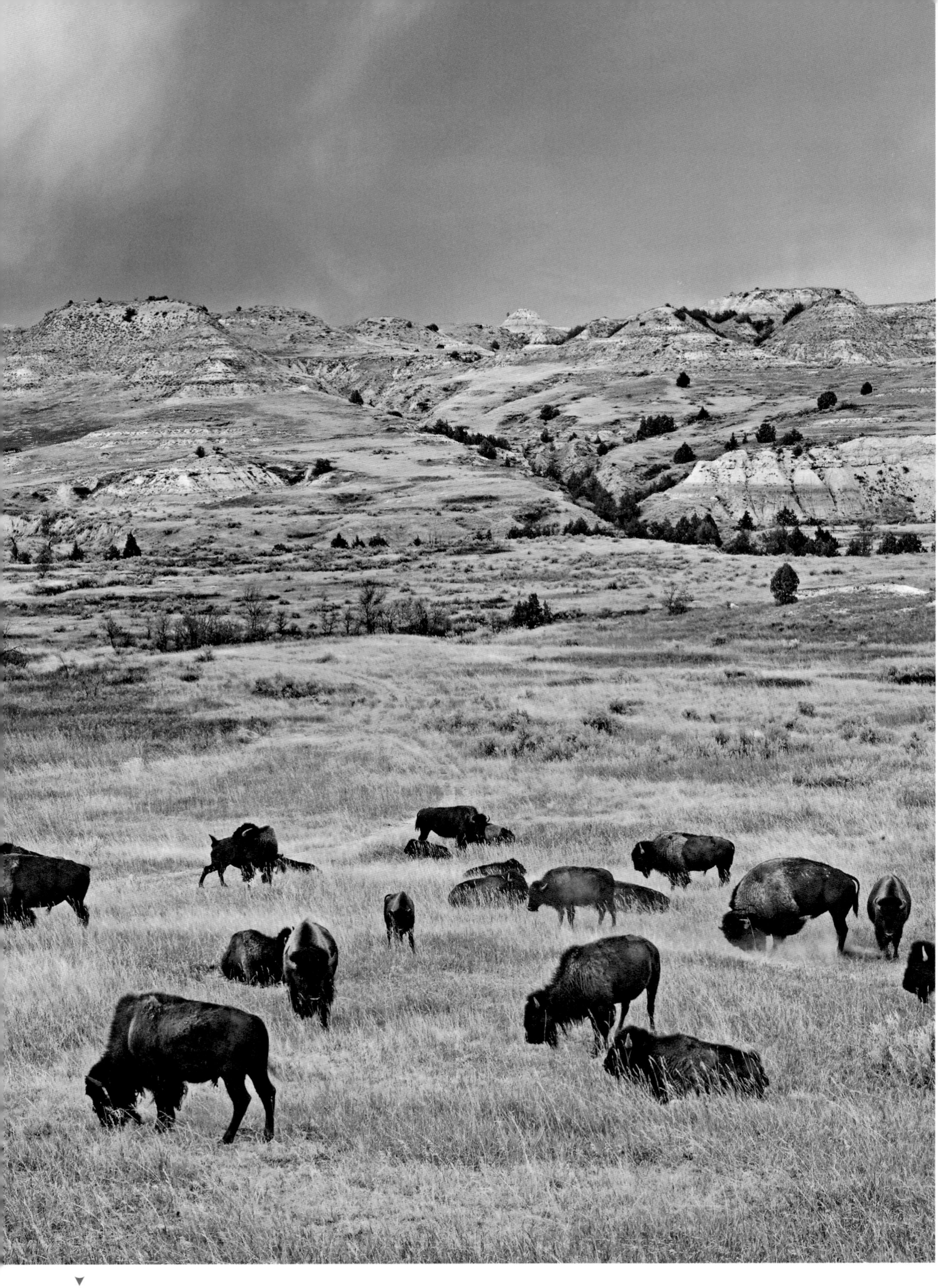

▼
A herd of bison graze near Scoria Point.

STORY AND PHOTOS BY
TIM FITZHARRIS

THEODORE ROOSEVELT

THIS LAND OF "VAST, SILENT SPACES" INSPIRED AMERICA'S BULL MOOSE TO BEGIN SAVING WILDERNESS TREASURES.

LOST IN THE VAST Great Plains in western North Dakota, Theodore Roosevelt National Park encompasses 70,467 acres of protected prairie wilderness. Here deer and antelope play, delighting wildlife photographers like me.

Described by its namesake as "a land of vast, silent spaces," the park extends a modest welcome to visitors at first, with an undulating expanse of green.

But look closer: This serene land is gouged by a mysterious badland architecture of jumbled gullies, valleys, buttes, pinnacles and spires painted with a truly remarkable color palette.

The Little Missouri River links the two main sections of the park. Its waters support trees and shrubs that make this expanse of pristine wilderness a hot spot for viewing wildlife.

Teddy Roosevelt traveled to Dakota Territory from New York to hunt bison in 1883, but he found that their once-great numbers had dwindled quite alarmingly. As he spent more time in the region, he grew more concerned about the damage to the land and the loss of wildlife.

His observations from that trip shaped a conservation policy that benefits America to this very day.

Theodore Roosevelt National Park is the largest protected mixed-grass prairie ecosystem in the U.S. It is home to bison, wild horses, elk, bighorn sheep, white-tailed and mule deer, prairie dogs and nearly 200 species of birds, including golden eagles, sharp-tailed grouse and wild turkeys.

Wildlife photography is challenging if you are intent on capturing a shot of a special bird or drawing close to the wary pronghorn or wild horses. But the bison, elk and deer are accustomed to people, and I shoot them at my leisure right out the side door of my motor home. I can grab close-ups of wildflowers, cacti and small critters like chipmunks and prairie dogs by hiking numerous trails.

Both sections of the park also offer scenic drives that allow for easy wildlife observation and panoramic views up and down the Missouri River valley.

In May and June, a trio of attractions lures me here with my camera—lush prairies dotted with wildflowers; frisky

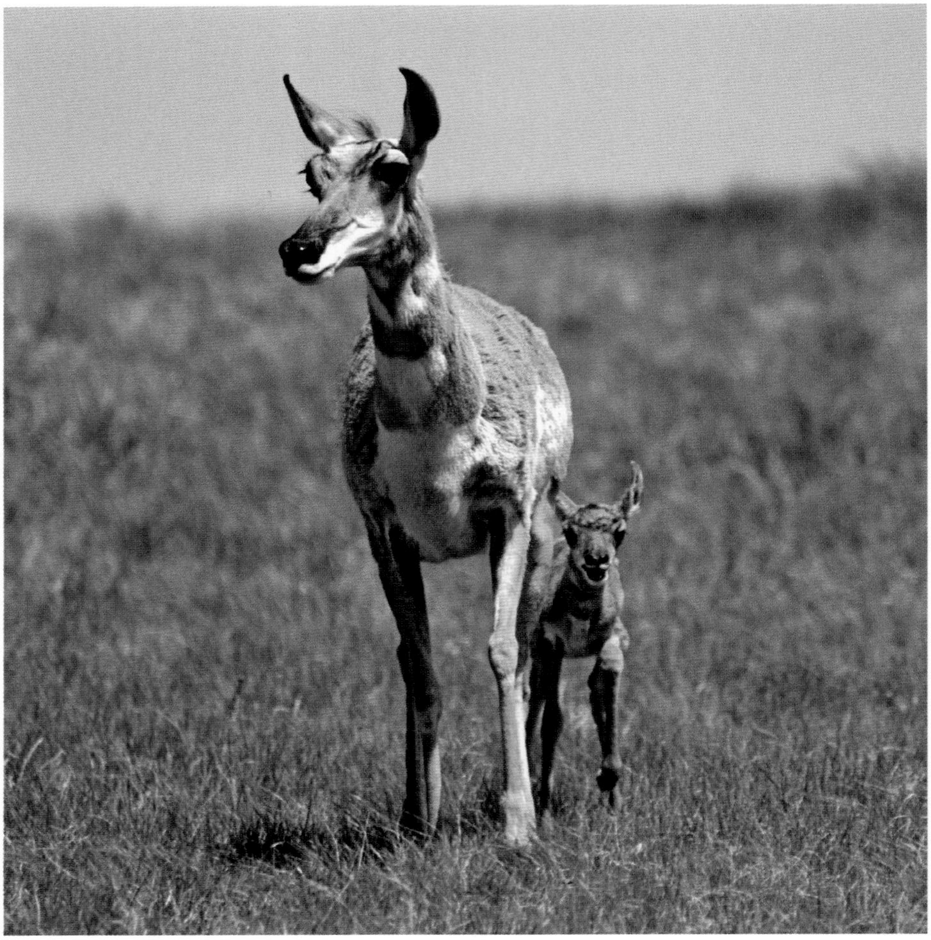

This sanctuary shelters many species of wildlife, like pronghorns.

POINTS OF INTEREST

NOT TO BE MISSED

Make sure to stop by Elkhorn Ranch Site. Theodore Roosevelt once considered it his home ranch. Now, only the foundations are still standing.

If you're a birder, you'll want to take a trip to the park during spring or fall migration. According to NPS, more than 186 species of birds, including sandhill cranes and warblers, either live in the park year-round or pass through on their yearly journeys.

FUN FACT

While in Mingusville, 35 miles west of Medora, Theodore Roosevelt once got into a bar fight! He didn't start it, of course, but he certainly finished it.

NEARBY ATTRACTIONS

Stop by the North Dakota Cowboy Hall of Fame in Medora to learn more about the state's rich western heritage; the 15,000-square-foot space hosts traveling and permanent exhibits. And there's a gift shop, too.

newborn bison, pronghorns and prairie dogs; and thunderstorms that light up the sky.

July marks the beginning of the bison rut, when gigantic bulls bellow, plow up the prairie with horns and hooves, and battle one another in dust-raising head-to-head battles.

September offers the nicest weather, with fair skies and mild temperatures that provide relief from the sweltering humidity of August.

While the scenery and wildlife bring in plenty of photographers, the park's well-preserved attractions, including Roosevelt's original ranch cabin and several Civilian Conservation Corps projects—a legacy of the other President Roosevelt, FDR—appeal to history buffs.

In and around the restored frontier town of Medora, museums, displays, live theater and historic sites provide insight into the challenges of settling this wild country.

Tales of legendary personalities like the Marquis de Mores, a French entrepreneur who named Medora after his wife, make the past come alive.

Medora offers plenty of shopping, restaurants and lodging, but I prefer to remain in the park's campgrounds, surrounded by nature, keeping my camera handy so I can capture each breathtaking detail of the High Plains. ■

Wind Canyon on the Little Missouri River.

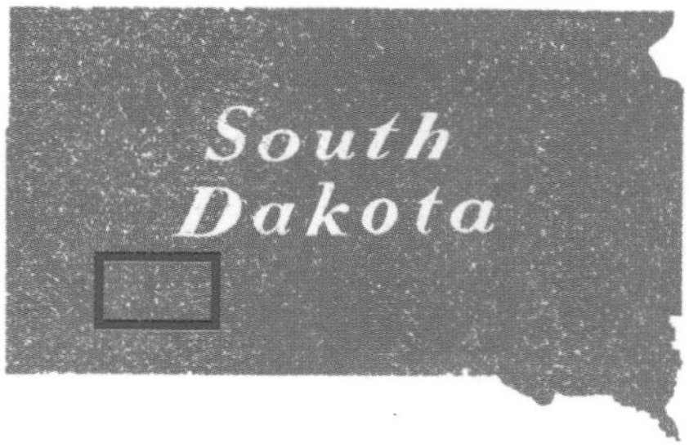

STORY AND PHOTOS BY
GREG LATZA

BADLANDS

MIGHTY ROCK FORMATIONS ATTRACT EVERYONE FROM FAMILY VACATIONERS TO STORM CHASERS.

MY FAMILY OFTEN CHOSE South Dakota's Black Hills for summer vacations and our excursions were never complete without a cruise along the 40 miles of Highway 240, commonly known as the Badlands Loop Road, which meanders through Badlands National Park.

Since the late Cretaceous Period, multiple layers of seafloor mud, river bottom sediment, tropical swampland and volcanic ash compressed upon each other and created formations of sedimentary rock. The Cheyenne River watershed drained this very erodible area and formed the rough, dried-mud terrain and jagged valleys that are the Badlands' signature.

I loved the drive, but most of our time there was in afternoon, along with thousands of other tourists. It wasn't until a few years later that I understood the true mystique of the Badlands occurs at the beginning and end of the day—times when the landscape comes alive with color.

Warm-colored sunlight, mixed with the various striations of colored earth, creates a palette of hues. In spring, the formations are dressed with emerald grasses that contrast against the warm earth tones. In fall, the dying grasses amplify the same warm tones and create a rich burst of yellows, oranges and reds. Set against a blue sky, the color contrasts can be almost startling.

My favorite addition is a prairie thunderstorm. Nothing adds more drama than thunderheads rolling across the horizon. Getting in position for a fast-moving storm front is more a matter of luck than planning. But, oh, what rewarding photos might occur—lightning strikes, rainbows and retreating cloud banks painted pink and orange by the sunset are just a few of the side benefits of Badlands thunderstorms.

My advice to Badlands newcomers? Try being there for the first or last hour of daylight, and avoid the flat midday sunlight. And if you see dark colors on the radar headed that way? Step on it!

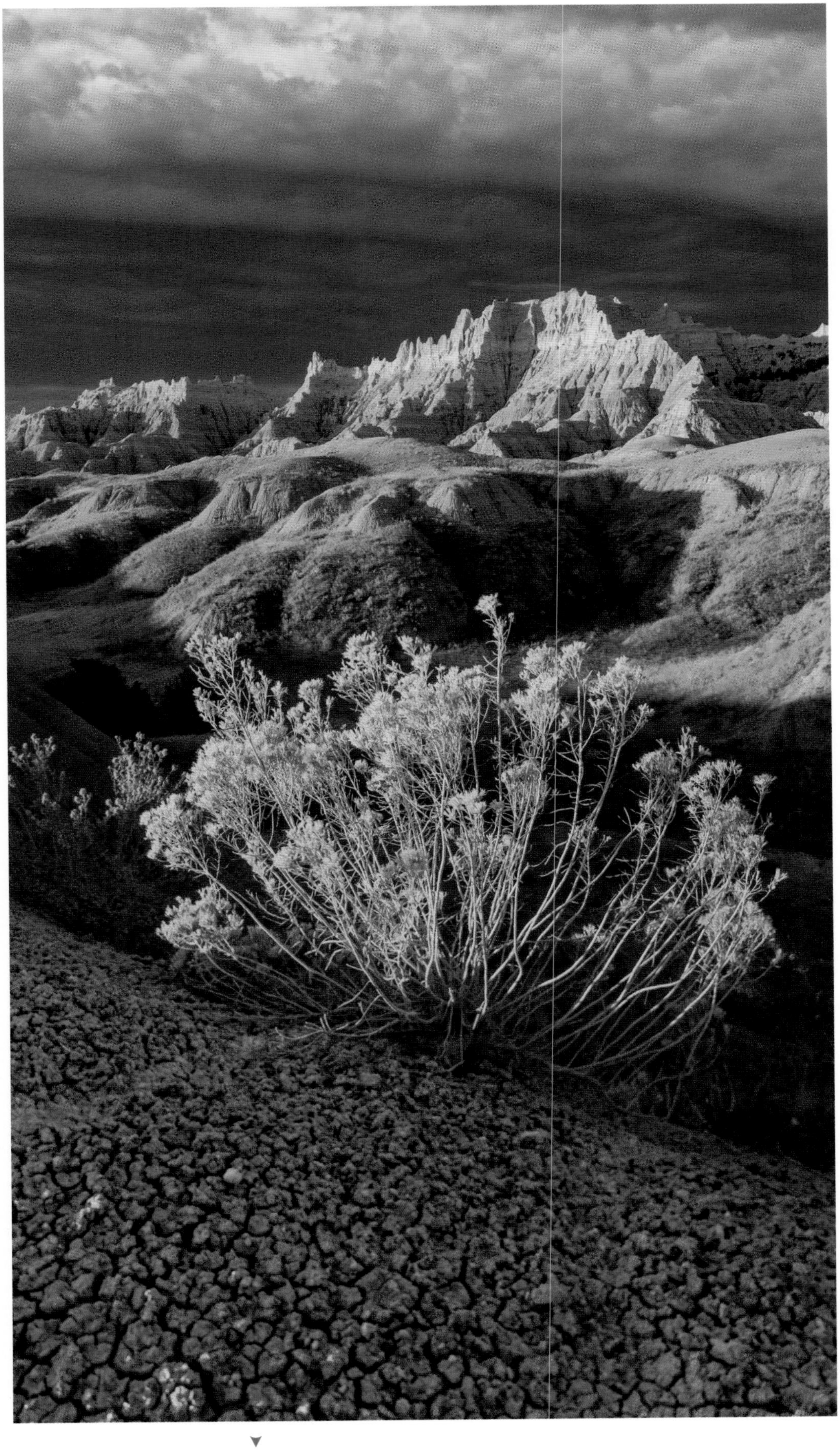

▼
Early morning sunlight casts the Badlands in warm, colorful hues.

POINTS OF INTEREST

NOT TO BE MISSED
Make sure to check out the Ben Reifel Visitor Center at the park's eastern end. The center offers museum exhibits where visitors can discover more about the park's history, as well as a fossil preparation lab and a 25-minute film about the park.

FUN FACT
The name "Badlands" honors the Lakota people, who lived on the land and referred to it as *mako sica*, which means "bad lands." When you imagine having to travel over the jagged cliffs and vast, waterless prairies by foot or in a wagon, it's not hard to imagine why early settlers would've thought the name was fitting.

WORDS TO THE WISE
Rattlesnakes call the Badlands home, but they're usually hiding during the day. To make sure you don't disturb them, don't stick your hands or feet in shady places or areas with limited or obscured visibility.

STORY AND PHOTOS BY
CHUCK HANEY

APOSTLE ISLANDS

EXPLORE A WORLD OF MAGICAL SEA CAVES, OLD LIGHTHOUSES AND MARITIME TREASURES TUCKED INTO LAKE SUPERIOR.

PADDLING A SEA KAYAK through Lake Superior to the islands at Wisconsin's northern tip had been on my bucket list for a long time. So I was excited about getting to spend the majority of a week getting to, camping on and exploring the wilds of the Apostle Islands National Lakeshore.

Eighteen of the park's 21 islands boast campgrounds. The chain also appeals to lighthouse lovers, with eight historic towers on six islands. But the highlight was the chance to paddle through the chain's fascinating series of sea caves, formed by wave after wave crashing into the islands' sandstone cliffs and carving out hollows barely big enough for a person to navigate a narrow kayak.

Our Devils Island campground was up on a bluff at the southern end of the island. A mile-long forest trail bristling with ripe blueberries led to an old lighthouse on the northern end. An older couple manned the structure in summer; it was delightful to visit and hear their stories and share a cup of coffee.

Winds mean everything here, and they're very unpredictable. One day I discovered that fierce winds kicking up whitecaps off the southern end of the island were totally blocked by the island itself. I rushed back to camp to tell my companions, and we were soon paddling calm waters on the island's leeward side, exploring the nooks and crannies of the handsomely eroded sandstone caves.

The best place to start exploring the Apostles is the charming town of Bayfield, with its many lodging choices and restaurants serving fresh local whitefish. Book a Lake Superior boat tour from here. I'm so glad I finally got to know Devils, Manitou, Sand and York islands—but there are many more lighthouses, magical caves and secluded sandy shores left for me to explore. ■

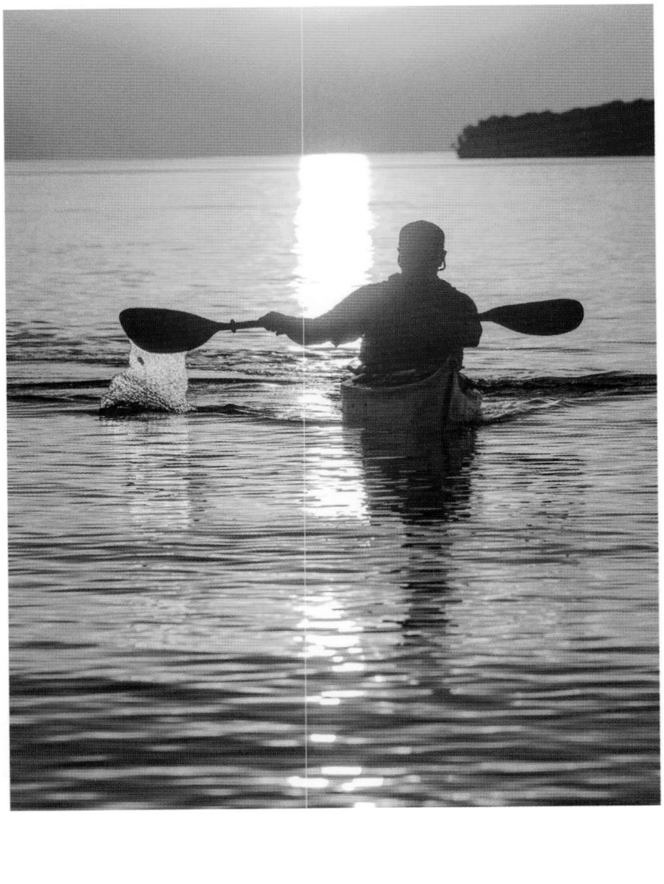

Top: *Wave-carved sea caves in the sandstone cliffs of Devils Island. Bottom: A kayaker enjoys a quiet Lake Superior sunset.*

POINTS OF INTEREST

NOT TO BE MISSED
Apostle Islands offers cruises that allow visitors to marvel at the beauty of the islands, the cliffs and the lighthouses from the water. The most popular cruise, according to NPS, is the Grand Tour, which takes visitors on a 55-mile journey through the heart of the archipelago.

FUN FACT
In the 1950s and '60s, the Apostle Islands were designated as one of the biggest migratory flyways in the Great Lakes region. Plenty of birds make their homes there, whether temporarily or on a permanent basis. One such bird is the endangered piping plover—just one of the shorebirds that can be found living around the islands.

WORDS TO THE WISE
If you're planning a trip to the islands specifically to visit the ice caves, be advised that a 2-mile round-trip hike on the ice of Lake Superior is required. In addition, the caves might not be open every year; park staff monitors them for safety.

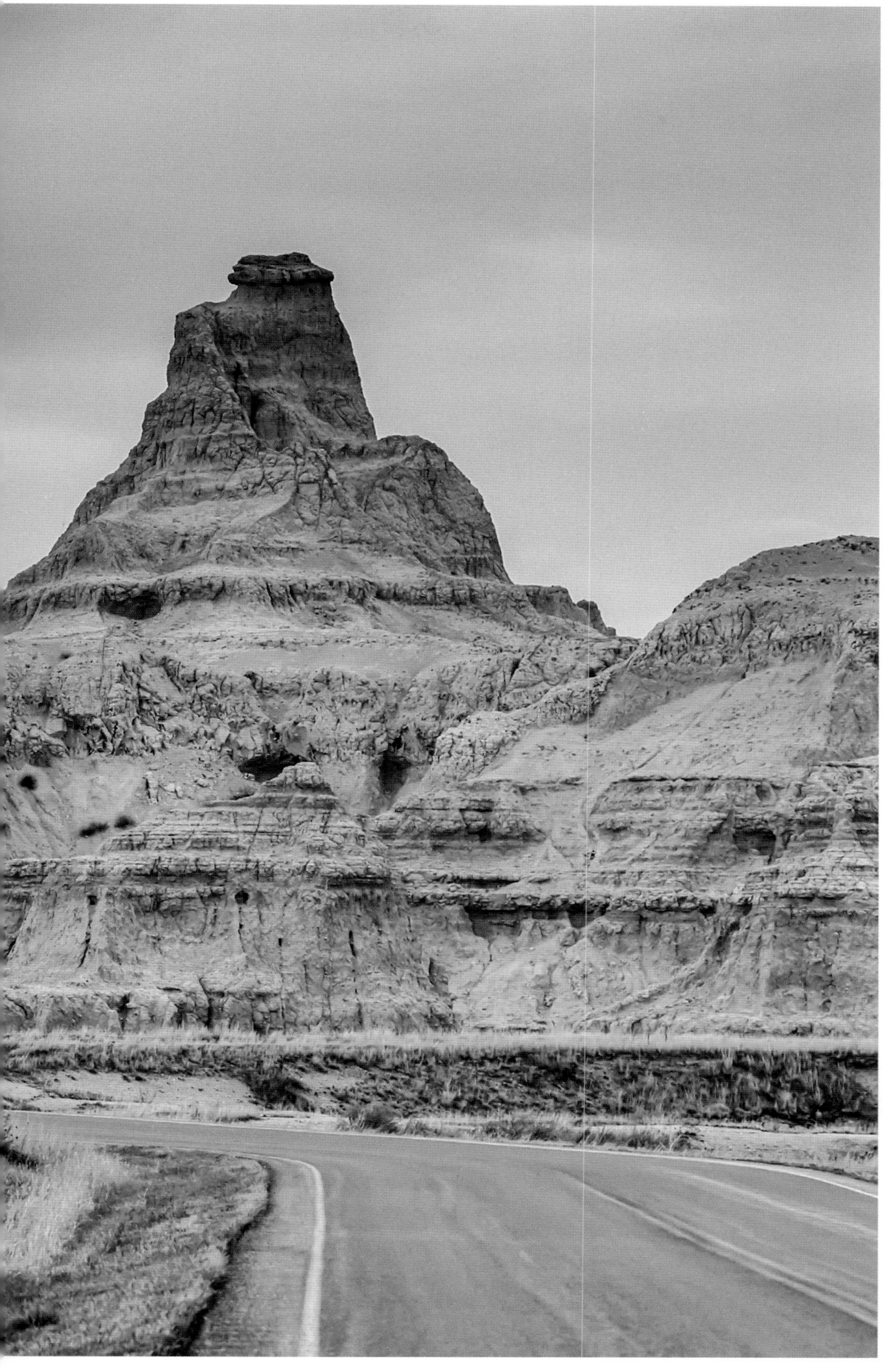

BADLANDS NATIONAL PARK

1936

Visitors enjoy traveling down the Badlands' winding road near the park's east entrance and taking in the scenery.

2016

Today, visitors still find joy in driving down the park's scenic routes—like Loop Road, pictured here. The road offers 12 scenic outlooks and plenty of chances to spot park wildlife.

THEN: GEORGE A. GRANT/U.S. NATIONAL PARK SERVICE; NOW: PETER UNGER/GETTY IMAGES

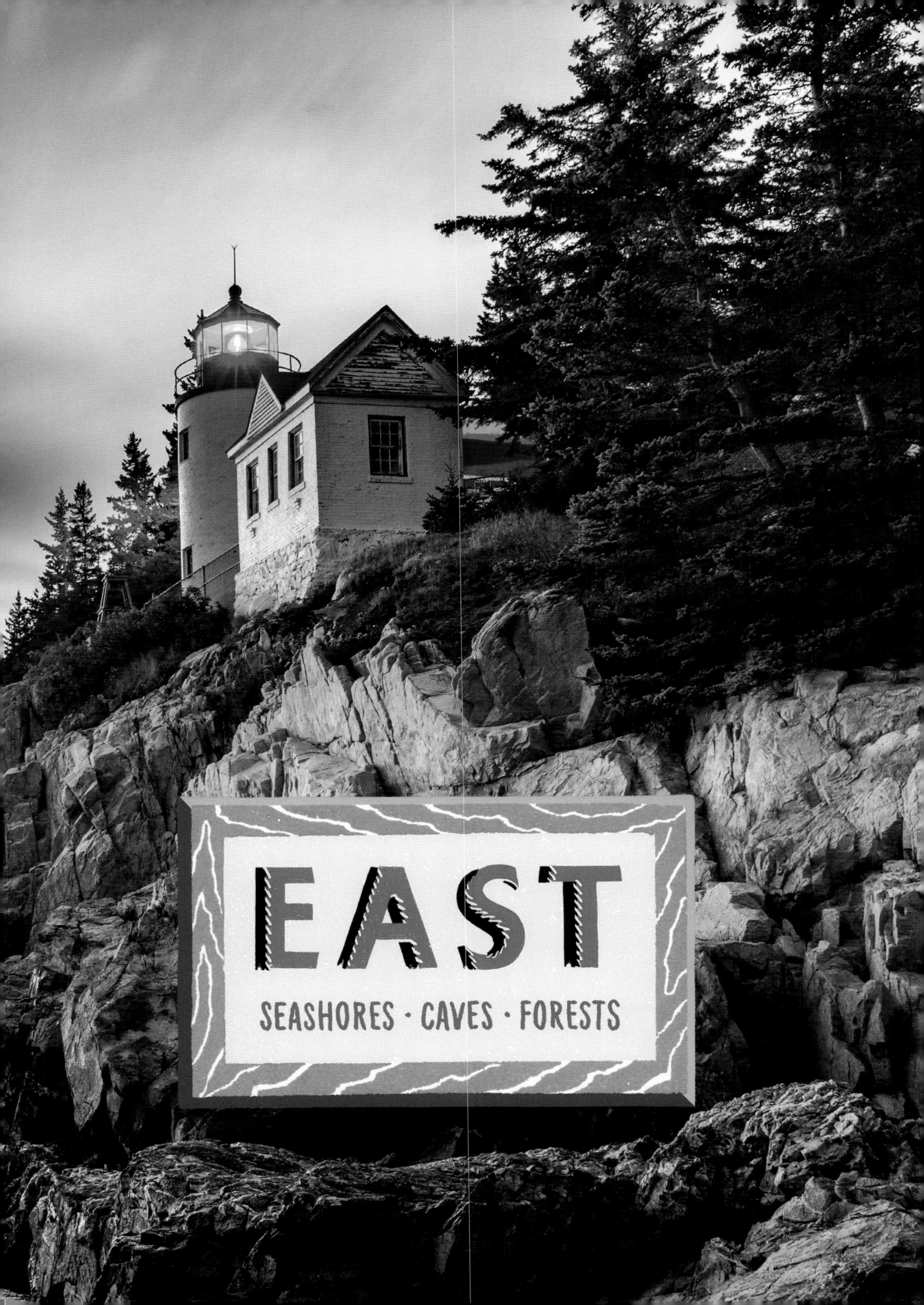

EAST

SEASHORES · CAVES · FORESTS

▼
Early morning at Eagle Lake.

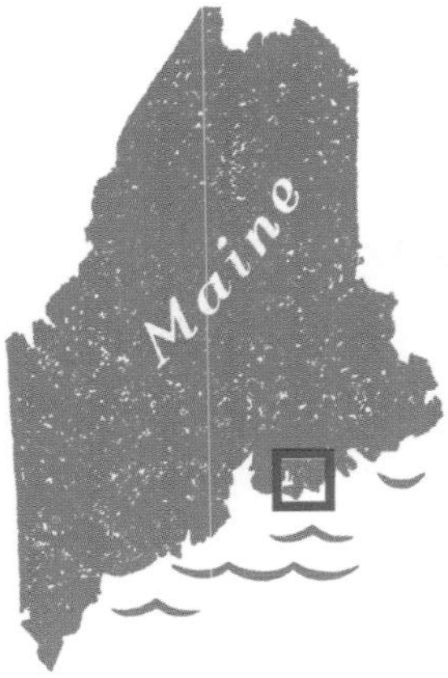

STORY BY **PAULETTE M. ROY**
PHOTOS BY **PAUL REZENDES**

ACADIA

FROM ROCKY COASTS TO MAGICAL FORESTS, YOU WILL CATCH YOUR BREATH AT EVERY TURN.

THE ALARM RINGS us awake at 3 a.m., and I give a little groan. Today my husband, Paul, and I are bound for Maine's Mount Desert Island, best known as home to Acadia National Park. Despite the early hour, we'll have plenty of company at our first destination: the top of Cadillac Mountain.

At 1,530 feet, this time-worn granite dome is the highest point along the North Atlantic seaboard, and from October through March it's the first place in the U.S. touched by the sun's morning rays. According to today's weather forecast, which calls for lowland fog and partly cloudy skies, we have the perfect conditions for a dramatic summer sunrise. Soon, despite the early hour, we're raring to go.

After a spectacular sunrise shoot, we pull onto Park Loop Road, which offers 27 miles of stunning scenery. But we drink in only part of it, making a detour for a 2-mile hike down Ocean Path, which skirts the rocky coastline. Between the trail and the waterline, a sprinkling of stepping-stone boulders offers a more adventurous route. The path ends atop 110-foot Otter Cliffs, one of the highest headlands along the eastern coast.

West and inland, the Jordan Pond House Restaurant is a tradition, not just for its famous popovers but for its scenic view overlooking the pond. We intend to stop and take a break from photography. But with the North and South Bubble Mountains casting reflections across the water, we can't resist taking a few more photos. Then, all too soon, it's time to move along.

We haven't planned our afternoon itinerary in advance, and now we pause. If this were autumn, there would be no shortage of inland waters hugged by foliage—scenes that simply take your breath away as the million hues of summer greens burnish into autumn's vivid golds, russets and reds. Our personal favorites are Duck Brook Bridge and New Mills Meadow Pond.

Asticou Azalea Gardens offers the same spectacular show, but we prefer to stroll its winding paths in spring, when we can gaze at endless shades of pink, orange and red blooms reflected in the placid pond as birds serenade us

One of six carriage road bridges.

POINTS OF INTEREST

FUN FACTS

There's no shortage of ways to appreciate nature in Acadia. This park—one of the top 10 most-visited in America—boasts 27 miles of historic motor roads and 158 miles of hiking trails.

If you're determined to spot wildlife on your visit, check out the "Tour de Wildlife" page on Acadia's website. There you'll find which trails not to miss.

WORDS TO THE WISE

You can bring your pet to Acadia! Plenty of hiking trails (more than 100 miles) allow pets on a leash no longer than 6 feet.

SIDE TRIP

Visit Maine Coastal Islands National Wildlife Refuge for more opportunities to hike shorter trails and bird-watch.

NEARBY ATTRACTIONS

Several museums are located in the area around Acadia, including the Mount Desert Oceanarium and the Great Harbor Maritime Museum.

with their sunny songs. More than 80 avian species call the gardens and its surrounding area home.

Today being a warm summer day, however, we turn south for a drive along Northeast Harbor. With his Portuguese sailor's blood, Paul can't help pausing to check out the sailboats before we head back north. Sargent Drive follows the shore of Somes Sound, a narrow, 7-mile body of water that nearly bisects the island.

Route 102 circles the western peninsula of the island, known as the "quiet side," an easygoing escape from the busier parts of the islands, like Bar Harbor. You won't find the typical tourist amenities here, but you also won't find traffic, overpriced food or crowded hiking trails. Instead, fishing villages, farmland, peaceful coves, picturesque harbors and scenic roads fill the landscape.

We reach the north end of the Sound at Somesville, the oldest settlement on the island. We pause to photograph the famous white wooden walking bridge and colorful flower boxes. Down and around to Southwest Harbor, we detour onto the shore-hugging southern Route 102A loop. Mansett treats us to fields of lupines arrayed before an Atlantic Ocean backdrop.

Further south, we pass Wonderland, a magical forest where silvery moss drips from spruce boughs as the path leads you through a long and shady corridor before opening to a dazzling view from the coast. In autumn, the forest's huckleberry bushes blaze a fiery red. Next up is Bass Harbor, shared by the charming fishing villages of Bass Harbor and Bernard, and the historic Bass Harbor Head Lighthouse perched atop its rocky cliff.

After all this, we hurry back to Cadillac Mountain to grab a sunset from a different vantage point. Satisfied but exhausted, I sigh. Another 3 a.m. wake-up will come much too soon. But as I watch the sun disappear, I think it can't come soon enough.

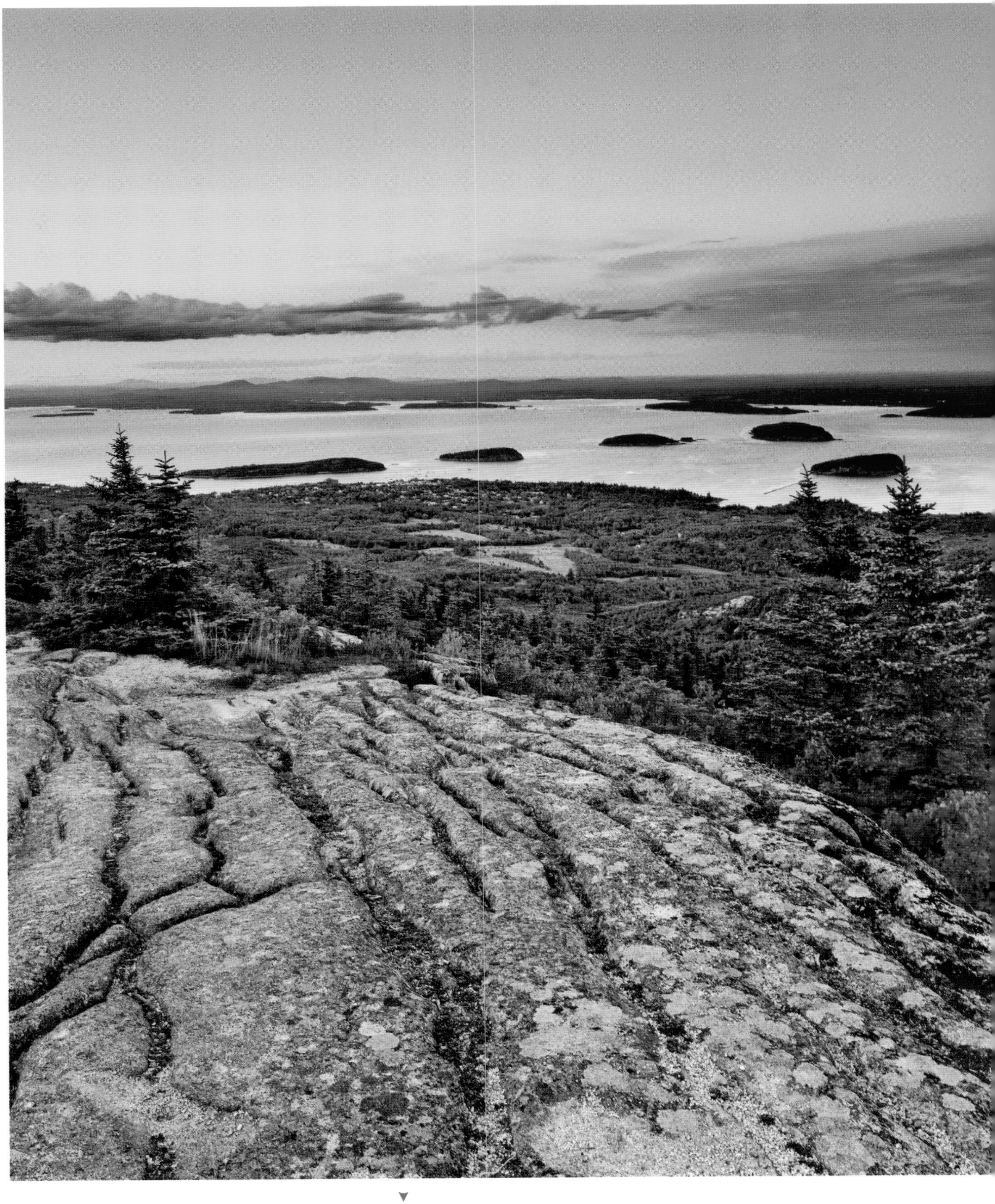

Bar Harbor and Porcupine Islands, as seen from Cadillac Mountain.

▼
Bearfence Mountain on the Appalachian Trail.

STORY AND PHOTOS BY
PAT & CHUCK BLACKLEY

SHENANDOAH

PICTURESQUE FARMS, MISTY MOUNTAINS AND HISTORIC SITES AWAIT IN VIRGINIA'S LEGENDARY VALLEY.

WE WERE BORN AND RAISED in Virginia's beautiful Shenandoah Valley, and we consider ourselves blessed to live here.

According to legend, the name Shenandoah derives from a Native American word that means "clear-eyed daughter of the stars." With its gentle mountains, rushing waters and green meadows, the spot fits its name well.

Nestled between the Blue Ridge and Allegheny mountains, the valley lies in the Shenandoah River watershed. Isolated from the rest of the Virginia colony by the Blue Ridge Mountains, the valley remained largely unsettled by Europeans until the early 1700s, when farmers of German and Scots-Irish descent began making their way from Pennsylvania in search of land suitable for farming. English settlers from the coastal Tidewater region followed in the mid-1700s.

These early settlers discovered fertile soil, a moderate climate, and abundant rainfall, wildlife and natural resources. Their farms yielded bountiful crops of grains and vegetables; their orchards produced bushels of peaches and apples. Sheep and cattle fattened in lush green pastures.

Today, many valley residents earn their living on family farms established by those who came before, growing the same crops and raising the same livestock. Agriculture is an important part of the regional economy: Four of Virginia's top five agricultural counties are in the Shenandoah Valley, and numerous small farms grow vegetables and fruits to sell at farmers markets. In season, especially in Mennonite country, roadside stands sell melons, corn, strawberries and other produce.

The region is also one of the nation's largest exporters of apples. When the orchards bloom in spring, it's a truly awesome sight. Known as Virginia's apple capital, the city of Winchester celebrates its agricultural heritage every April and May by hosting the Shenandoah Apple Blossom Festival, an immensely popular weeklong event that draws thousands. This family-friendly fair features music, dancing, an arts and crafts show, parades and a carnival.

In addition to agriculture, the valley brims with history. There are plenty of museums and other sites to explore. One favorite is Winchester's Museum of the Shenandoah Valley, which features a multitude of interesting exhibits that tell stories of the valley and its residents. Another is Staunton's Frontier Culture Museum, which features a complex of original and reproduction 17th and 18th century farmsteads from England,

The Baylor Mill in Swoope.

POINTS OF INTEREST

FUN FACT
Shenandoah National Park blooms with abundant flora and wildlife. Skyline Drive runs through the park for 105 miles, with numerous overlooks along the way.

SIDE TRIP
Natural Bridge State Park is home to a 215-foot limestone arch that once was owned by Thomas Jefferson. The 1,500-acre state park is also a National Historic Landmark.

NEARBY ATTRACTIONS
The Museum of the Shenandoah Valley in Winchester has many exhibit-filled galleries. On the grounds is the Glen Burnie House, built in 1794 by Winchester's founder, James Wood. Six acres of gardens surround the house.

Luray Caverns are the largest caverns in the eastern United States. Visitors follow lighted, paved paths through cathedral-sized spaces, which rise 10 stories high, to see massive stone formations.

Ireland, Germany and West Africa. The West African farmstead is based on an Igbo household in land that is now Nigeria, home of some 40 percent of enslaved people brought to Virginia. Here, visitors will learn about their origins, customs and contributions to American culture.

Of course, the best way to get to know and appreciate the beauty, history and friendly people of the valley is to travel its roads and visit with folks. There are many scenic drives that take it all in, especially in the spring.

Skyline Drive, in Shenandoah National Park, is one of them. Its 105-mile route offers a bird's-eye view of the valley from the park's overlooks. There, visitors can enjoy springtime blooming flora and watch for fawns and black bear cubs.

We love looking for wildflowers along the park's 500-plus miles of hiking trails, including a 100-mile section of the famous Appalachian Trail. These trails also lead to the park's stunning waterfalls, which are at their best in the spring.

At Waynesboro, Skyline Drive ends, but the road continues as the Blue Ridge Parkway, winding 469 miles through the Blue Ridge Mountains all the way to the Great Smoky Mountains National Park in North Carolina.

The area west of the little town of Dayton is home to a Mennonite community. We love driving the back roads and admiring the tranquil beauty of this area, with its tidy farms and pretty white houses, handsome barns, silos and grazing cattle. We always welcome and return waves and smiles from the occupants of the horse-drawn buggies we pass.

Another fantastic drive is U.S. Route 11, which takes you through the valley's past and present. This road—the main highway through the valley before construction began on Interstate 81 in the late 1950s—has a long, storied history. Once a Native American trail, it became the Great Wagon Road, used by early settlers making their way to the western frontier. Now known as the

Valley Pike here in Shenandoah, the road opened up travel and commerce, and was a key transportation route for both the northern and southern armies during the Civil War.

Connecting the towns of Winchester, Harrisonburg, Staunton and Lexington, Route 11 passes through charming villages and gorgeous countryside with idyllic farms and grazing livestock.

Like Skyline Drive, Route 11 is scenic in the spring, with lambs and calves frolicking in intensely green pastures; farmers on tractors plowing up rows of rich, dark soil; and blooming dogwood, redbud and fruit trees painting the hillsides, with those blue mountains standing as a backdrop. The air is filled with the smells of mown hay and turned soil. During this time, puffy clouds float from the west in a magical, turquoise blue sky.

This drive is like a trip back in time, passing by old stagecoach stops, taverns, mills and covered bridges and Civil War battlefields and museums. Of special interest is the Virginia Museum of the Civil War in New Market.

On May 15, 1864, New Market saw the arrival of 257 cadets from Virginia Military Institute—the youngest of whom was just 15. Having marched 85 miles from their school in Lexington, they joined the forces of Gen. John Breckinridge. Ten of them died and 45 were wounded, including Chuck's great-great-uncle.

Each year, people come from all over the country to take part in the New Market battle reenactment. Held on the weekend closest to the battle's anniversary, the event is the longest

Virginia's Dark Hollow Falls are a short 1.4-mile round-trip hike off Skyline Drive near Big Meadows.

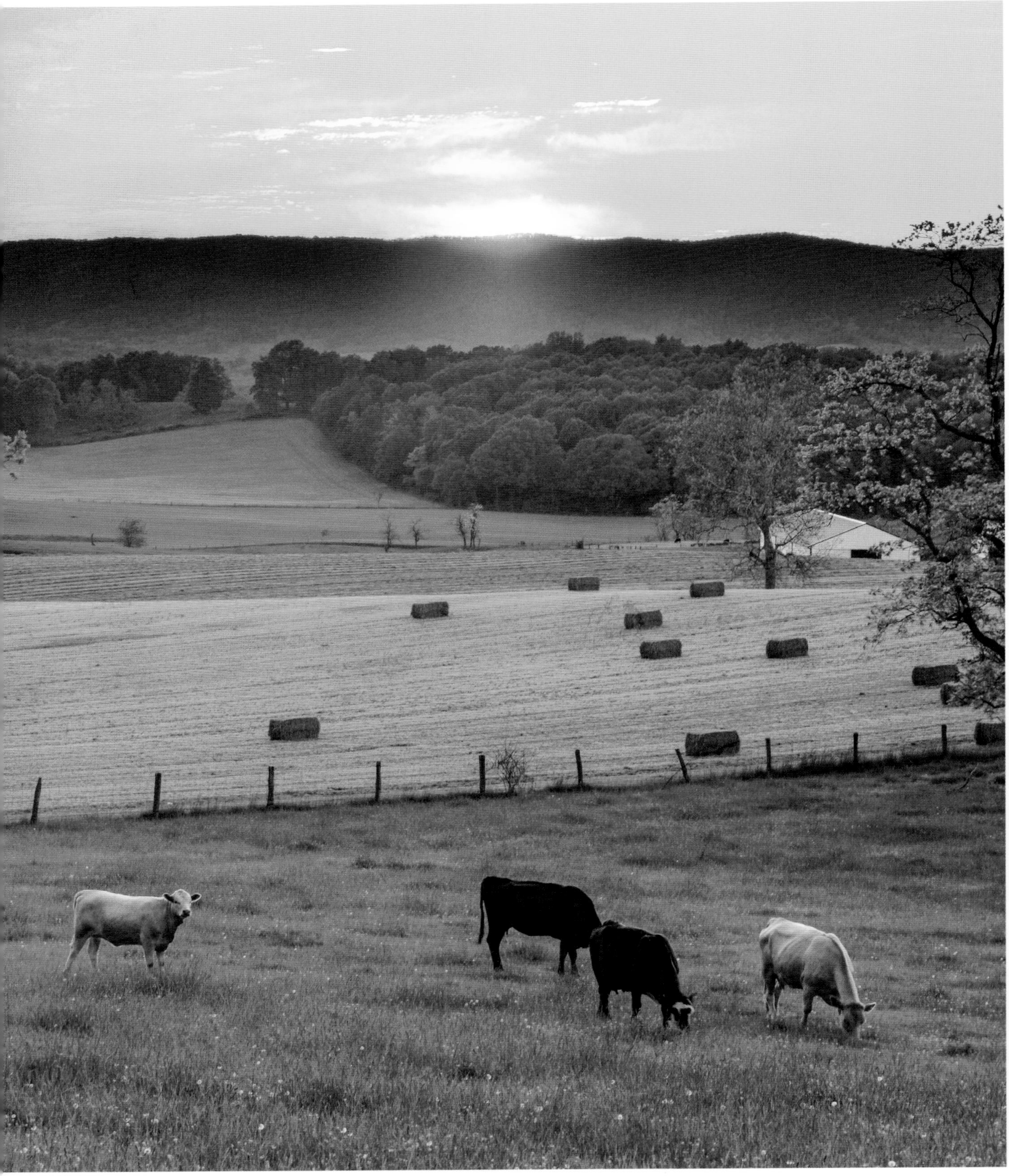

▼
Lush pastures make for a tasty dinner near Middlebrook.

Autumn's sunrise glows bright at Shenandoah National Park.

continual reenactment in the United States that is still held on the field where the battle was fought.

In Rockbridge County at the southern end of the valley, Route 11 crosses over the Natural Bridge of Virginia. This National Historic Landmark in a state park is a 215-foot mammoth limestone arch that once belonged to Thomas Jefferson, and George Washington claimed to have surveyed it when he was a young man.

The valley's cities and towns feature lovingly restored structures from the 18th, 19th and early 20th centuries and numerous historic sites. In Winchester, visit both a log cabin that briefly served as an office for George Washington, and the house Stonewall Jackson used as his headquarters.

About 95 miles south is the small city of Staunton, birthplace of President Woodrow Wilson and the location of his Presidential Library and Museum. Lexington, further along Route 11, is a historic college town with many Civil War sites. Everywhere you go in the valley, there's a history lesson waiting to be learned.

Perhaps our beautiful valley's greatest assets, however, are its residents. They are incredibly warm, friendly, kind and generous, as well as hardworking, industrious and always eager to help a neighbor or a stranger in need. When out photographing one day, Chuck got his Jeep stuck in a ditch. A passing farmer stopped and, after assessing the situation, told him he'd be back in a jiffy.

He went down to his farm and returned shortly with a winch that he used to pull the Jeep out. Chuck thanked him, and the gentleman just told him he was glad to help. That's typical in these parts.

For those of us who call it home, the Shenandoah Valley is truly God's country. From its gentle, misty blue mountains, picturesque farms and lively towns to its exciting history and wonderful people, it's a little slice of heaven, and there's no place we'd rather be.

STORY BY
DANA MEREDITH

CONGAREE

EXPLORE HISTORY AND NATURE IN A PARK THAT HAS SUPPORTED LIFE FOR 13,000 YEARS.

GAZE SKYWARD through towering bald cypress, loblolly pines and tupelo trees in the middle of the largest and tallest old-growth bottomland hardwood forest east of the Mississippi. The cacophony of buzzing insects, croaking frogs and hooting owls is joined by the rustling of turkeys, deer and wild boar in the brush. The amazing biodiversity of Congaree National Park reveals itself in nearly 27,000 acres of flood plain 20 minutes east of Columbia.

This free park is not a swamp, but the nearby Congaree and Wateree rivers flood around 10 times annually, leaving behind nutrients that refresh this eerie ecosystem. Check the Harry Hampton Visitor Center for trail maps and current conditions.

Hike the easy 2.4-mile Boardwalk Loop Trail through the forest, or take the Weston Lake Loop Trail around the lake. Explore the Cedar Creek Canoe Trail in your canoe, or paddle the 50-mile Congaree River Blue Trail from Columbia to the park.

From mid-May to mid-June, Congaree hosts one of only three species of synchronous flashing fireflies in North America. Check with the park for dates and times of the annual Fireflies Festival.

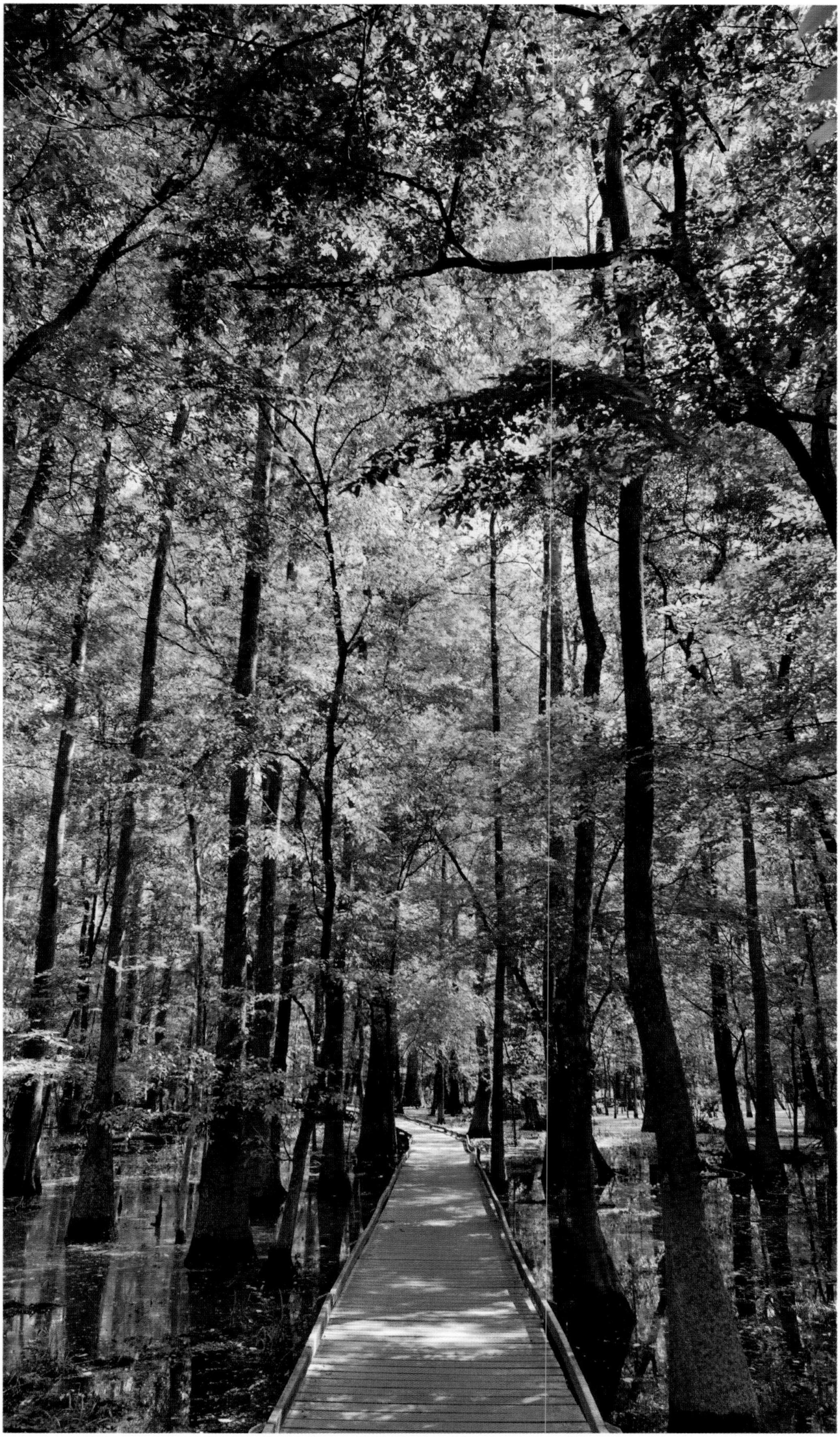

▼
Bald cypress trees reach for the sky along Boardwalk Loop Trail.

POINTS OF INTEREST

NOT TO BE MISSED

If you enjoy canoeing or kayaking, you'll want to check out the Congaree River Blue Trail. This paddling path stretches from the state capital, Columbia, to Congaree National Park and provides access to several hiking trails.

If you're looking for the best views in the park, check out the Boardwalk Loop Trail (2.6 miles) and the Weston Lake Loop Trail (4.4 miles).

WORDS TO THE WISE

Planning to make the trip for the Fireflies Festival? The best time to see the bright bugs is between 9 and 10 p.m. Dogs aren't permitted on the Fireflies Trail.

SIDE TRIP

While you're in South Carolina, consider heading to Fort Sumter and Fort Moultrie National Historical Park, about 100 miles southeast. There, you can learn about the forts' American Revolution and Civil War history.

STORY AND PHOTO BY
PAT AND CHUCK BLACKLEY

MAMMOTH CAVE

DESCEND INTO A GARDEN OF EDEN AT THIS PARK WITH HUNDREDS OF CAVES AND PLENTY OF HIKING.

THIS DESTINATION IS KNOWN for over 400 miles of caves, but there's also much to see aboveground, and in mid-April, the Cedar Sink Trail is a wildflower enthusiast's dream. At first we found the hike there to be pleasant, but a bit unremarkable. Then, after descending into a large depression, we arrived at a platform and gazed down into a Garden of Eden.

Filled with native trees and lush vegetation, the sink was surrounded by cliffs of layered sandstone and limestone. A stream emerged from a cave and babbled on the surface before disappearing into another cave. The forest floor and cliff faces were draped with colorful wildflowers.

Well-kept paths wind through large clumps of red and nodding trilliums, blue phlox, larkspurs, fire pinks, yellow celandines, Dutchman's breeches and more. Hikers can reach the floral wonderland by way of a 1.6-mile loop trail that's rated moderate, although there's a steep set of stairs to the sink. The reward is absolutely worth taking the climb.

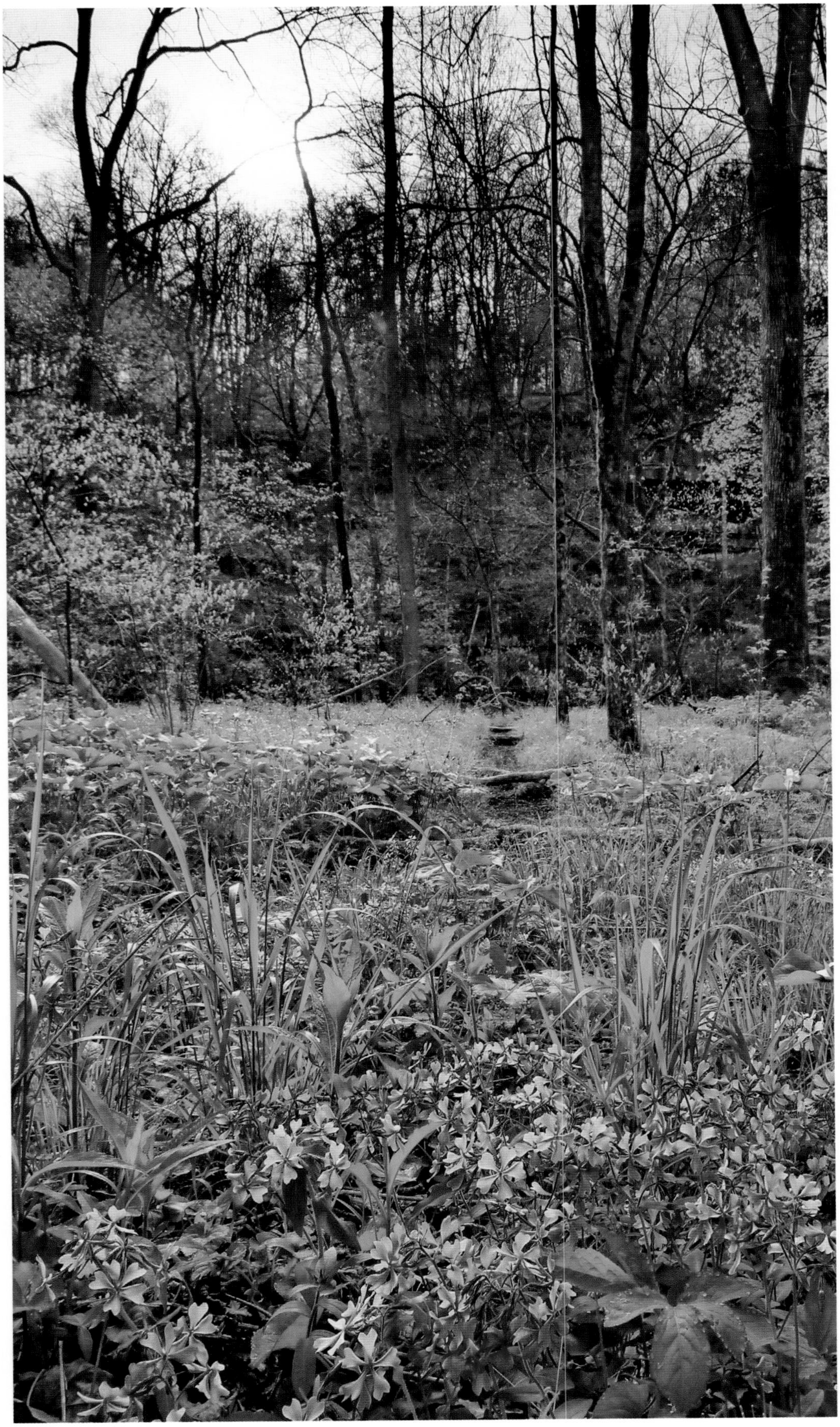

▼

Delicate phlox and trilliums decorate the Cedar Sink at Mammoth Cave.

POINTS OF INTEREST

FUN FACTS

During the War of 1812, the mineral saltpeter was mined from the caves to use in black gunpowder. Today, visitors can see remnants from Mammoth Cave's mines, including vats and wooden pipes.

Visitors can explore several historic churches and cemeteries at Mammoth Cave. Some churches are open, inviting visitors to imagine what life was like for settlers in the area.

SIDE TRIP

Mammoth Cave is located less than an hour away from Abraham Lincoln Birthplace National Historical Park. There, visitors can step inside the Memorial Building, constructed where the Lincoln cabin is believed to have been built.

NEARBY ATTRACTIONS

Close-by towns and communities offer plenty of chances for dining, lodging and exploration; Bowling Green, Brownsville, Cave City and more are all a short drive from the park.

1.

2.

3.

1. BEAUTY ALL AROUND
Roughly a 3-mile round-trip hike in Shenandoah Valley leads you to the summit of Sharp Top Trail, near Bedford, Virginia. It's the perfect place to behold amazing 360-degree views. –**ASHLEE NEMETH**

2. CHANGING SEASONS
I took this photo at an entrance area to Great Smoky Mountains National Park near Bryson City, North Carolina. Gorgeous fall colors are reflected in the water, a calming reminder of the beauty that occurs here every year. –**ANTHONY GIACOMINO**

3. A SURPRISE VISITOR
While driving in Great Smoky Mountains National Park, I am typically moved by the beauty of the mountains, waterfalls and wildflowers. But to my surprise I spotted this bull elk in the Oconaluftee River. –**CINDY YOUNT**

4. GLORIOUS NEW DAY
This photo showcases the serenity of an early morning sunrise as witnessed atop the summit on Cadillac Mountain in Acadia National Park. –**TODD ERB**

4.

1. 

2.

3.

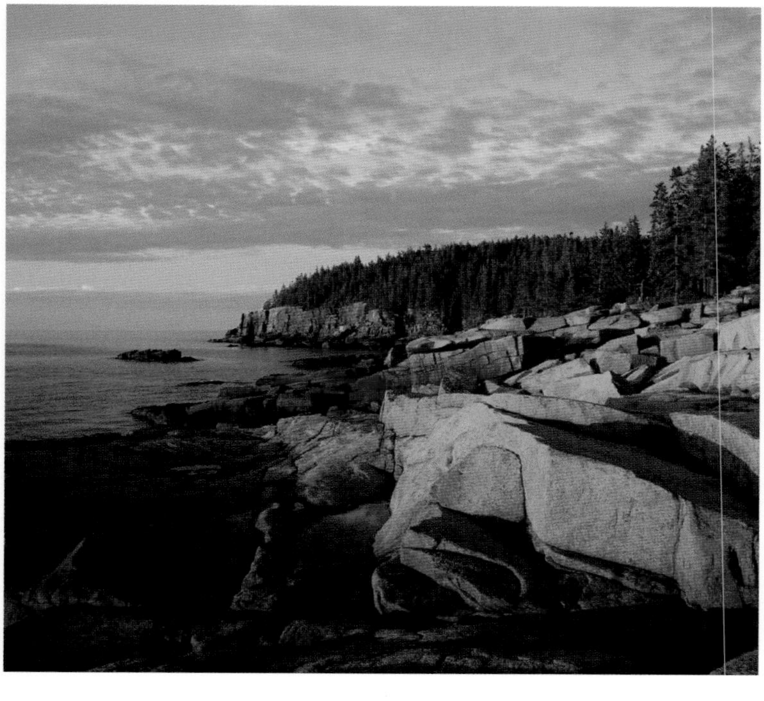

4.

1. NATURE'S MAJESTY
My family and I visited Acadia National Park in Maine last summer. The beauty and untouched nature was so overwhelmingly breathtaking.
– **KELLY DEAN**

2. INNER PEACE
This is the type of sunset we get in Everglades National Park. The calm water transports me to a quiet place and reminds me it's going to be OK.
– **JESSE WILSON**

3. PERFECT PICTURE
While heading home after an amazing day at Cades Cove in the scenic Great Smoky Mountains, we spotted this lone coyote. – **BARBARA HOUSTON**

4. FIRST RAYS OF LIGHT
Catching the sunrise in Acadia National Park is a popular activity, as it offers the first sight of the sunrise in the continental United States (at least for part of the year). It is always beautiful.
– **KAREN CHRISTMAN**

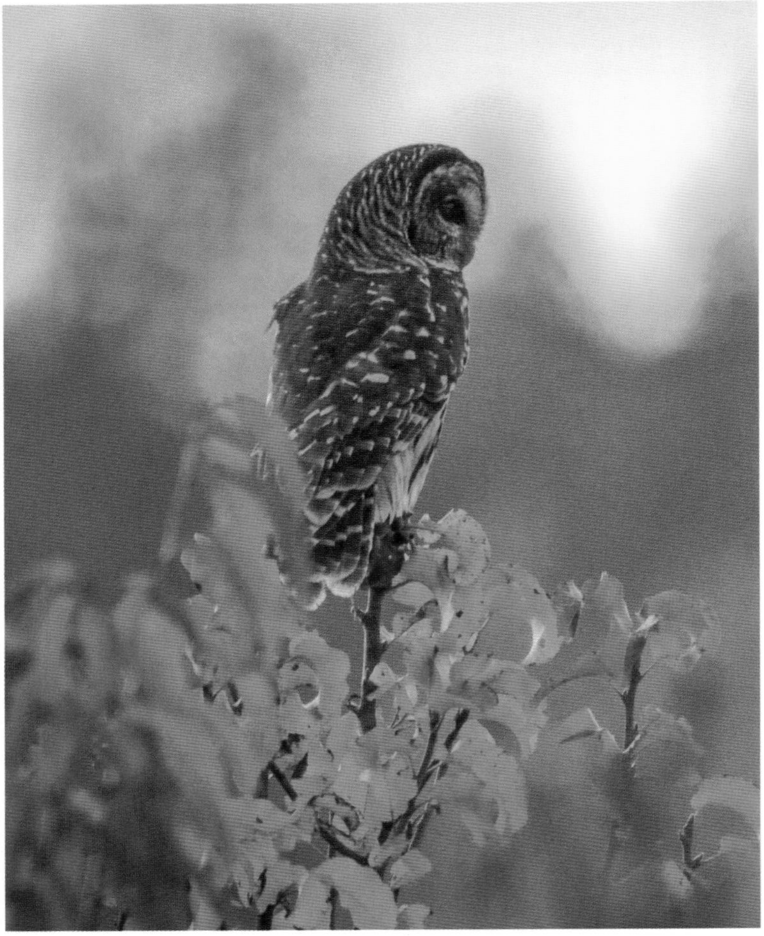
1.

1. *WHOO* IS IT?
This gorgeous barred owl resides right outside Congaree National Park in South Carolina. I carefully approached the field where the bird sat to photograph it in the setting autumn sun.
– **DANIEL RIDDLE**

2. GORGEOUS AND GREEN
I took this photo at the Great Smoky Mountains in May. I am amazed by the beauty of the many trails throughout the Smokies—more than 800 miles of them. – **PATTY BARNES**

3. ACADIA'S SPLENDOR
This photo is of Jordan Pond in Acadia National Park, Maine. The greens and blues are truly magnificent; this park and the state of Maine have so much loveliness to offer. – **BRIAN WILLEY**

4. IN THE MOMENT
While my vacation in Virgin Islands National Park was incredible, I found it challenging to live in the moment. One morning, while snorkeling with my husband, all the fish seemed to disappear. As I looked around, I was shocked to see this turtle gracefully swim by. It reminded me of how small my problems were and put things into perspective for me. – **LEAH NICHOLSON**

5. THE END OF A BEAUTIFUL DAY
I captured this stunning sky at Bar Harbor in Acadia. There are many excellent places to watch the sun set in the park. – **MIKE COHN**

2.

3.

4.

5.
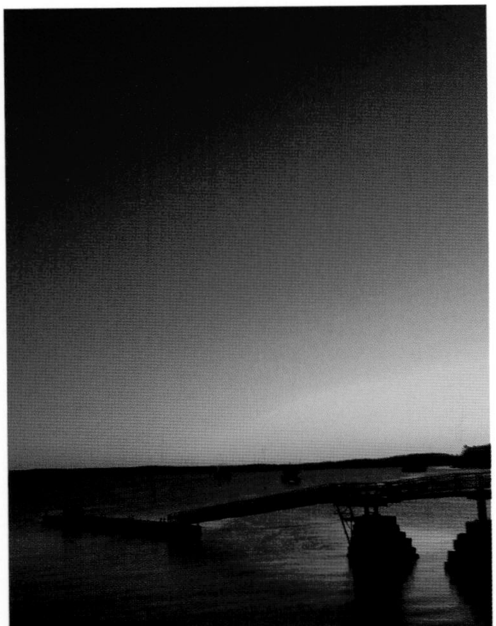

▼
Waterfall at Hot Springs National Park.

STORY BY
DONNA B. ULRICH

HOT SPRINGS

ARKANSAS' RESTORATIVE SPRINGS GAVE BIRTH TO STATELY BATHHOUSE ROW IN THE GOLDEN ERA OF "THE AMERICAN SPA."

FOR THOUSANDS OF YEARS, Native American tribes gathered in what some called the "Valley of the Vapors," searching for relief from common ailments through soaking in mineral-rich hot springs. In modern times, the area has become a mecca for people "taking the waters" in Hot Springs, Arkansas.

Early European settlers came to the waters at Hot Springs Mountain in hopes of relieving problems ranging from sinus, muscle and joint pain to afflictions of the skin. They built simple platforms over the outflow to inhale the vapors.

Crude brush huts and log cabins came next, and, as the place known as "the American Spa" grew in popularity, bigger and better accommodations sprang up. Today a row of luxurious stone and masonry bathhouses beckons visitors at Hot Springs National Park.

The natural thermal springs are fed by ancient rainwater filtering down to areas deep in Earth's crust, where it's slowly heated. Then it rapidly rises to emerge from 47 local springs as steaming-hot water.

Congress first gave federal protection to the area's natural features in 1832, 40 years before Yellowstone became the first national park. Designated as Hot Springs National Park in 1921, it is the smallest in the park system. The promenade, called Bathhouse Row, was constructed by wealthy entrepreneurs and is preserved as a National Historic Landmark District to provide a peek into the city's grand past.

And a colorful past it was! Gambling, prostitution and bootlegging were as much a part of everyday life in this peaceful valley as the spas. Las Vegas-style amenities and a secluded location attracted gangsters from the late 1800s to the mid-1900s.

Al Capone used the remote town in the Ouachita Mountains as a base for making and shipping moonshine during Prohibition. Hot Springs and its surrounding forest provided cover for the stills; from there Capone struck deals to ship the contraband to his clubs in Chicago.

National Park Ranger Coby Bishop, born and raised in Hot Springs, worked

The Arkansas wilderness at twilight.

POINTS OF INTEREST

FUN FACTS

The springs in the park are all grouped around the base of Hot Springs Mountain. They release a flow of over half a million gallons of water every day.

You might think of Hot Springs for its waters, but it's a notable archaeology site as well. People have been on the park's land for more than 10,000 years.

WORDS TO THE WISE

Forgot your water bottle? You can drink the water at Hot Springs. At the thermal and cold spring fountains, you are able to fill up jugs of drinking water from the springs.

NEARBY ATTRACTIONS

There are plenty of museums and things to do in the city of Hot Springs. One notable attraction is The Gangster Museum of America, which features exhibits about mobsters who used the springs.

in the park for six years. "I loved the variety of architecture," he says. "Each of the bathhouses reflects the builder's sense of style. My favorite was the Maurice, because of its simple yet elegant lines, beautiful tile work, Mediterranean style and spectacular stained-glass skylights and windows."

Concessionaires run the bathhouses, with payment made to the federal government for the spring waters, which are now considered recreational rather than therapeutic in nature. Renovations continue.

The Buckstaff, which has operated continuously since 1912, and Quapaw are still open for a relaxing soak and spa experience. The Fordyce now is the national park's visitor center, and the Ozark Bathhouse currently houses the Museum of Contemporary Art.

The surrounding Ozark landscape features 26 miles of trails meandering through oak, hickory and pine forests.

Spring is an especially lovely time, with wildflowers, azaleas and flowering dogwoods brightening the lovely forest. Hikers might even come across a natural cold spring and easily forget that a bustling city is just out of sight.

In that sense, Hot Springs is ideal both for "taking the waters" and taking in the history that endures.

LEFT AND RIGHT: ZRFPHOTO/GETTY IMAGES

▼
A stone bridge in the Gulpha Gorge Creek.

▼
The hike to Lynn Camp Prong is an easy one with huge rewards.

STORY AND PHOTOS BY
PAT AND CHUCK BLACKLEY

GREAT SMOKY MOUNTAINS

SOMETIMES HAVING THE GREAT SMOKY MOUNTAINS TO YOURSELF MEANS RISING BEFORE THE SUN.

THE GREAT SMOKY MOUNTAINS have captivated us for more years than we would admit. Nonetheless, we never tire of the misty mornings in its coves, the explosion of rhododendron bloom along its streams or the riot of fall color among its trees.

Affectionately called the Smokies, this mountain range is mostly preserved within the 800-square-mile Great Smoky Mountains National Park, straddling the Tennessee-North Carolina border. The Cherokee called these mountains "place of the blue smoke" in tribute to the mist that perennially envelops the landscape here.

However, the very things we love about the place beckon the masses. Today, with 11 million visitors per year, the national park is one of the most-visited in the country. Over the years we have learned that the best time to avoid the crowds is the early morning, as the park and its wild residents awaken to a new day.

When we want a quiet vacation, Chuck and I head over to Townsend,

POINTS OF INTEREST

NOT TO BE MISSED

Known for lovely wildflowers in the spring, Greenbrier is rarely crowded. The hike along Porters Creek Trail is a colorful wildflower trek that rambles past a historic log cabin and a barn.

At Foothills Parkway, west of Gatlinburg, you'll find more than 32 miles of scenic parkway stretching from Wears Valley to Chilhowee. The road boasts spectacular mountain views around every bend.

Discover Roaring Fork Nature Motor Trail, which was named for a loud and fast stream. This 5½-mile drive winds past clear streams, waterfalls and pioneer structures.

FUN FACT

In Elkmont, the clubhouse and cabins of the Appalachian Club still stand along with abandoned resort homes once frequented by the well-to-do from Knoxville. Remnants of logging operations here include an early 20th century railroad bed repurposed as a hiking trail.

Fog lifting at the Henry Whitehead Cabin.

Tennessee, which calls itself "the peaceful side of the Smokies." We find it true to its claim—and an ideal spot to dine, refuel and settle in for the night. From here, we can access the most beautiful spots on the Tennessee side of the Smokies without encountering the crowds a few miles away.

Townsend is not a village as much as it is a short and linear group of motels, restaurants and stores connected by a main road that is parallel to a well-maintained walking and biking path. We frequently see folks enjoying the path as the cool of the evening sets in. The town offers opportunities to tube or swim in the Little River, visit a cultural museum or explore caverns.

But it's the mountains we've come here to see. Staying in Townsend is most convenient to Cades Cove, our favorite spot in the park. Here, in this valley surrounded by high mountains, lived a community of pioneers who embodied the Appalachian spirit.

Today their churches, cabins and barns are preserved and their fields are still tended. We love stepping back in time in such a tranquil setting, which is one of the most popular places in the park.

We've found that Cades Cove is best visited early in the morning, so we line up at the entrance gate for the dawn opening to relish one of the valley's magical sunrises. In these early hours, fog usually drifts within the cove and wildlife is plentiful near the roads. It is typical to see deer sparring, turkeys strutting and, maybe, a bear browsing not far from our car.

After sunrise, we travel the mostly empty cove roads until midmorning or so, when visitors begin to flock in from

Gatlinburg, a tourist town known as the gateway to the Smokies. Since the early fog has dissipated and wildlife are back in the woods, it is now that we take our leave of the valley.

From May to September, Cades Cove is restricted to bicycle or foot traffic until 10 a.m. on Wednesdays and Saturdays. This is the best time to take your bike ride here. We aren't cyclists, so on these mornings, we have a lovely breakfast at our favorite place for old-fashioned country cooking: Riverstone Restaurant in Townsend.

At midmorning, we explore some of the park's more than 800 miles of hiking trails, including several former railroad beds that the hardworking Civilian Conservation Corps converted to trails in the 1930s. These hikes vary from strenuous mountain climbs to easy peaceful strolls. Whatever your skill level might be, each hike leads to breathtaking beauty.

The Little River Trail, our favorite repurposed railroad bed, follows its namesake east from Elkmont, a former logging camp. This gently sloping path passes beside the tumbling waters of the river as it flows through the heart of the Great Smoky Mountains.

With several places to turn around, this trail can be an easy, relatively short walk or a full day's trek through land that changes with the seasons: delicate wildflowers in springtime, colorful rhododendrons in summer and vibrant leaves in fall.

Also at the Little River trailhead, we have the option to change our course and follow the Jakes Creek Trail, which ascends the mountain to the Cucumber Gap Trail and its majestic stand of tulip poplar trees.

Closer to Townsend, at Tremont, is Middle Prong Trail, another converted railroad bed that follows the Middle Prong of the Little River. This is an easy hike of a half-mile to the Lower

White-tailed deer forage in the fields.

▼
Dawn breaks beside Sparks Lane in Cades Cove.

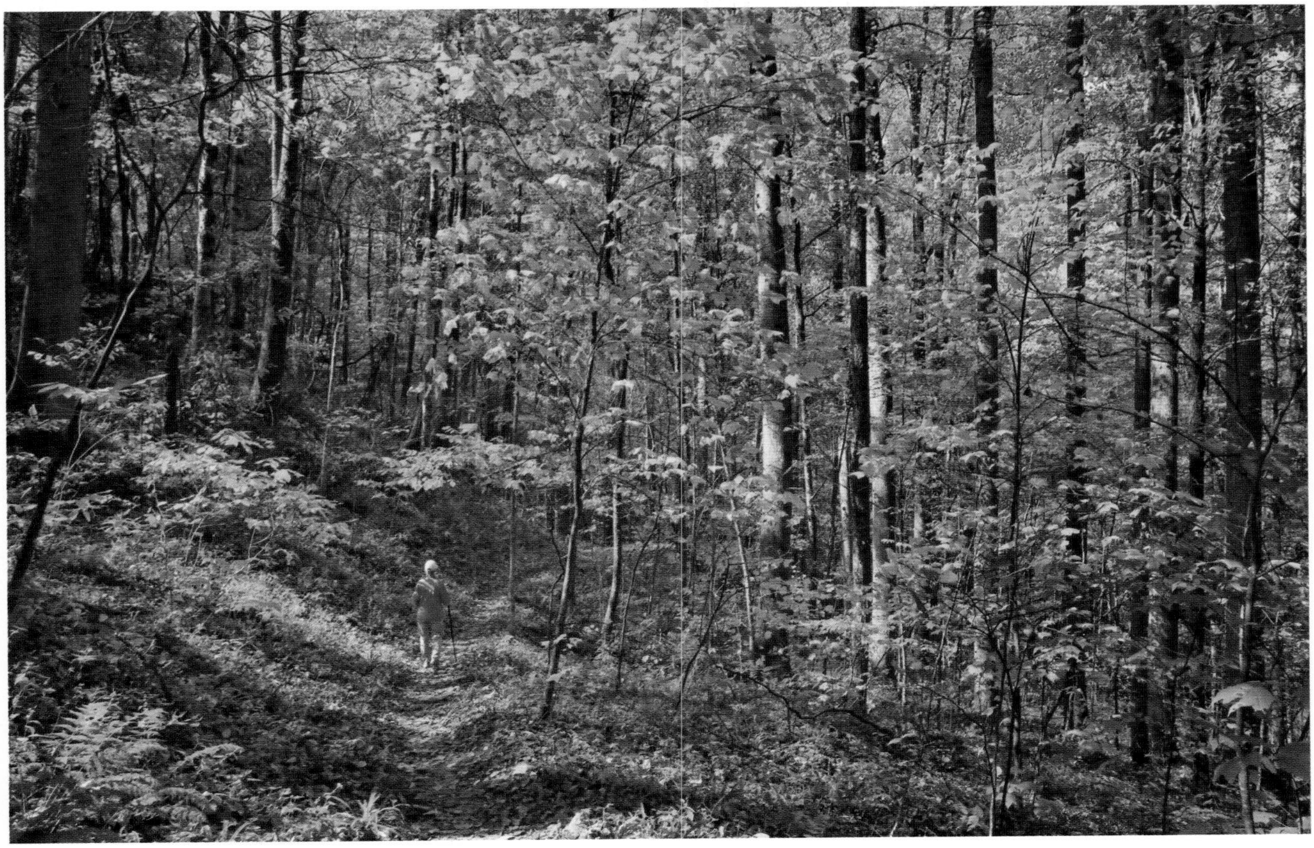

A hiker on the Cucumber Gap Trail treks past fantastic fall color.

Lynn Camp Falls, which cascade dramatically from the left. The trail extends beyond the falls at a steep grade for several more miles on the rail bed, then proceeds on a strenuous stretch up the mountain.

Even if we're not hiking, we find the drive to Tremont beside the Middle Prong—on a road that is half paved and half well-maintained dirt—to be among the loveliest in the park.

Another of our favorite midmorning destinations is Newfound Gap Road, which rises 3,000 feet in 14½ miles. While soon-to-be-bustling Gatlinburg is just beginning to yawn and stretch, we're admiring the park's famous overlooks, including Chimney Tops, a craggy bare double peak the Cherokee call Forked Antler.

If there is time, we drive the 7 miles to Clingmans Dome, the highest peak in the Smokies. Even if we don't hike the trail to the observation tower, the view from the parking lot is a must-see. By noon, the crowds arrive, and soon the overlook parking lots are filled.

Planning ahead, we picked up lunch in Townsend earlier so we can eat at a picnic area along the route. Our favorite is Chimneys, deep in the woods and not far from its namesake mountain on Newfound Gap Road. We find a spot near the stream and bask in the afternoon sunshine.

Knowing when and where to find peace and stillness makes the entire experience here just perfect for us. We hope you fall in love with the Smokies as we have.

STORY BY
CINDY JORDAN

CANAVERAL

EXPLORE AND SIGHTSEE AT CANAVERAL'S SANDY BEACHES AND IN ITS BLUE OCEAN WATERS.

THE SEA LURED US to Canaveral National Seashore, where we explored the 24-mile stretch of powdery white sand, laughing at funny little birds (sanderlings), running from the blue-gray waves and breathing in the salty air.

Home to more than 1,000 fish and bird species and even more plant and wildlife species, Canaveral sits on a barrier island complex. The Atlantic Ocean is on one side, the Indian River (really a lagoon) is on the other, and in between lies Mosquito Lagoon, which covers about two-thirds of the park.

We made our first stop at the Apollo Visitor Center, picked up a map, learned about the history of the island and set off to find the nesting sea turtles that lay their eggs under the sand.

My family and I scoped the dunes and peeked through railroad vines and sea oats, hoping to catch a glimpse. Then we turned to the lagoon, where turtles spend their adolescent years sheltered among the mangrove roots and seagrasses.

The waters are alive with oysters, clams, manatees, dolphins and more. At Indian River, the salty ocean water meets and mixes with fresh water. Such complex estuary ecosystems are often called cradles of the ocean because they're the spawning grounds for so much life.

With such beauty and abundance, I can see why the ancient Timucua tribe lived here. Archaeological sites, including Turtle Mound (one of the tallest Native American shell middens in Florida), abound.

Canaveral is a year-round destination with places to fish, swim, boat, canoe, camp or just relax on the beaches. There are no high-rise buildings, restaurants or cars, but paved roads and boardwalks lead to numerous historic sites, pristine beaches and hiking trails.

Today Canaveral National Seashore remains much as Mother Nature intended it to be—a peaceful refuge.

MICHAEL WARREN/GETTY IMAGES

A wooden boardwalk, among palmettos and sabal palms, leads to the Atlantic Ocean.

POINTS OF INTEREST

FUN FACT

Canaveral's name is one of the oldest geographical names on record in America. It means "place of Cane."

WORDS TO THE WISE

Look out for jellyfish! NPS warns that during the summer, men-of-war and jellyfish can wind up on the shore. They recommend carrying vinegar on the beach to use in case of a sting. Hot water (and an abundance of caution when walking) helps, too.

NEARBY ATTRACTIONS

You'll want to check out Kennedy Space Center on your trip, too. Featuring exhibits about everything from the moon landing to the next phases of space travel today—as well as the Astronaut Training Experience—the Kennedy Space Center is a must for anyone interested in exploring the stars.

STORY AND PHOTOS BY
MARILYN BAGGETT

EVERGLADES

FIND PEACE IN THE EVERLASTING BEAUTY AND ABUNDANT NATURE OF AMERICA'S LARGEST SUBTROPICAL WILDERNESS.

FOR MOST OF MY YEARS I have lived less than an hour away from an American treasure: the Florida Everglades. As I found my life increasingly stress-filled, I sought a place of solitude and beauty to revive my spirit.

One day, I recalled that Everglades National Park was near, so I ventured out with a full tank of gas, a light lunch, water, my camera, tripod and bug spray. What I found was a timeless place I had all but forgotten. My every sense was intrigued by the wonder and majesty of it all.

At first I felt the quiet, but I soon realized the air was alive with sounds and devoid only of the noise of people. The constant buzz of insects was topped with the cries of tropical birds. And the air vibrated with the grunts and bellows of the great alligators. My eyes feasted on sunsets, ablaze with pinks, oranges and reds, crowning the sawgrass prairie and the pineland forests.

During dry season flocks of birds, including iridescent purple gallinules, snowy egrets and roseate spoonbills, congregate around watering holes. In wet season I hear the low rumbling of thunder in the distance. Warmed by the sun and refreshed by the rain, the cycle of life here hangs in a delicate balance.

After each visit, I am renewed and ready to face any challenge. I'm so very thankful for those who possessed the foresight to protect and preserve such a rare natural wonder. I look forward to my next visit when I will once again find something new to appreciate in my big backyard.

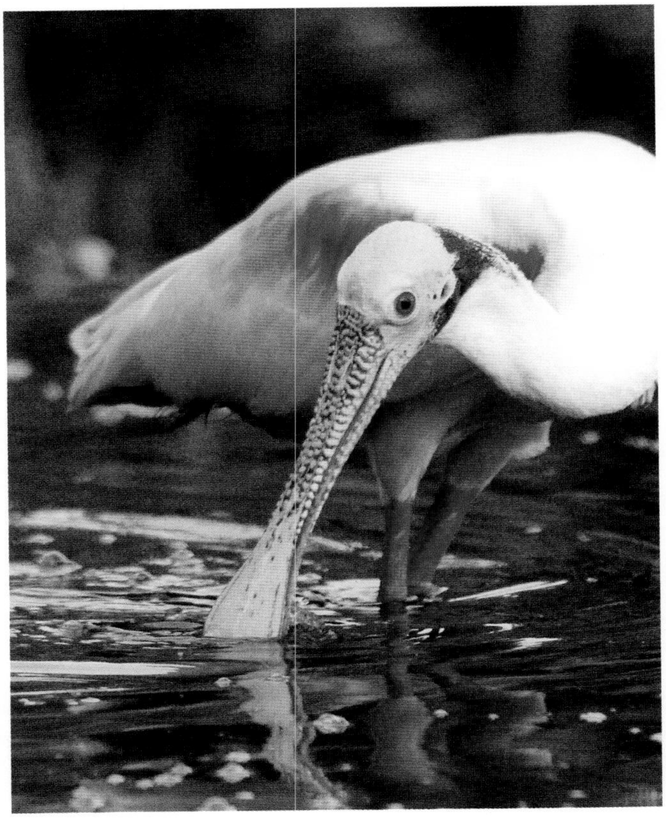

Top: Marilyn finds serenity in a cypress grove in Everglades National Park. Bottom: Roseate spoonbill.

POINTS OF INTEREST

FUN FACT

Many early national parks were founded to preserve scenery, but Everglades National Park was created to preserve habitat for a variety of animals. Residents include red and gray foxes and black bears, as well as birds like wood storks, herons and egrets.

WORDS TO THE WISE

Protect your car from vultures! NPS has let visitors know that vultures living in the park are often drawn to windshields and windshield wipers. To keep yourself from getting a nasty surprise when you return from your hike, the park service recommends using tarps and bungee cords to cover cars when parked; these items are available for free at some visitor areas.

SIDE TRIP

Take a day trip to Big Cypress National Preserve. Located just a half-hour away from the Everglades, it features plenty of opportunities for hiking, canoeing, stargazing and more.

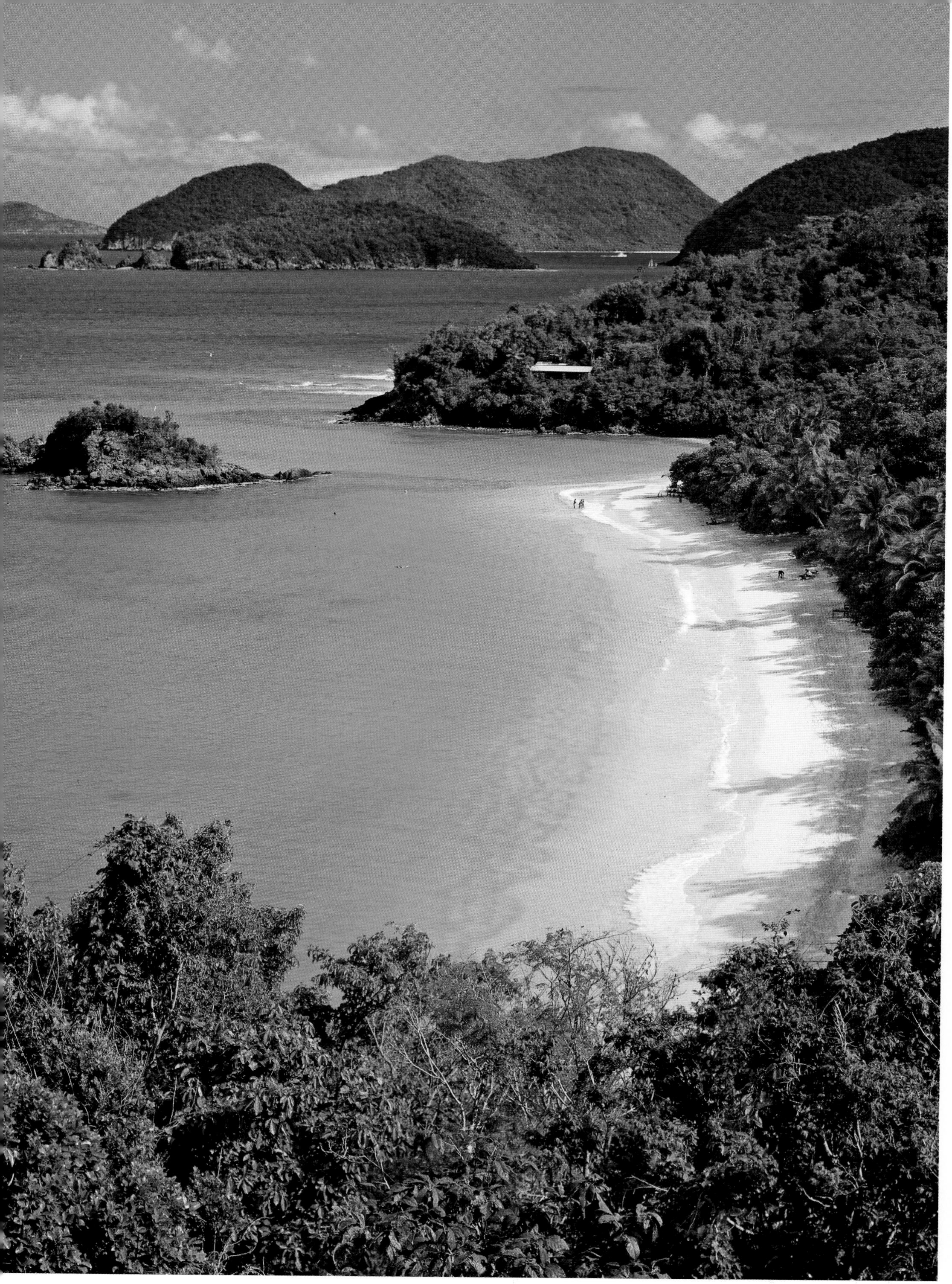

▼
Trunk Bay is the home of the park's underwater trail for snorkelers.

STORY BY **DONNA ULRICH**
PHOTOS BY **LARRY ULRICH**

VIRGIN ISLANDS

SNORKEL, SAIL AND SMILE IN A TROPICAL PARADISE WITH ONE OF THE WORLD'S BEST BEACHES.

YOU CAN DRIVE to most of America's national parklands, while some others require an airplane flight. But on our first visit to Virgin Islands National Park, we sailed in.

Located on St. John, in the Caribbean Sea, this treasure of the park system is a legacy of conservationist Laurance Rockefeller, who donated more than 5,000 acres for it in 1956. Park officials acquired 5,650 undersea acres off the northern and southern coasts in 1962, and today the park covers more than half of St. John's 19 square miles and nearly all of tiny Hassel Island.

Imagine a luxurious tropical paradise with easy access to beaches—and we own the place! The U.S. purchased St. John and many smaller islands from Denmark during World War I. Virgin Islands is one of just two national parks not located within the 50 United States, the other being the National Park of American Samoa in the South Pacific.

Weather in the park averages a balmy 79 degrees, with very little temperature change between summer and winter.

My husband, Larry, and I spent 11 memorable days exploring Caribbean waters on a 42-foot sailboat before anchoring off the park's Trunk Bay, consistently voted one of the 10 best beaches in the world. The long strip of white sand, framed by lush tropical plants, stretches invitingly for a quarter of a mile.

Offshore, an underwater snorkeling trail through the Caribbean invites the visitor to linger and enjoy dazzling coral formations and fish of colors unfamiliar in our terrestrial world. Signs along the 225-yard underwater path tell snorkelers about the coral and other life forms they may see, including the coral-munching parrot fish, moray eels and trumpet fish. Farther out in the bay you may see green turtles, stingrays and eagle rays.

Serious snorkelers can also explore many other interesting reefs and bays along St. John's north coast. In fact, coral reefs surround much of the island.

Though you can camp in the park, we hadn't brought the necessary equipment to do so. There are cottages available for rent, but we chose to rent a bungalow complete with resident anoles—quick-moving lizards that eat bugs.

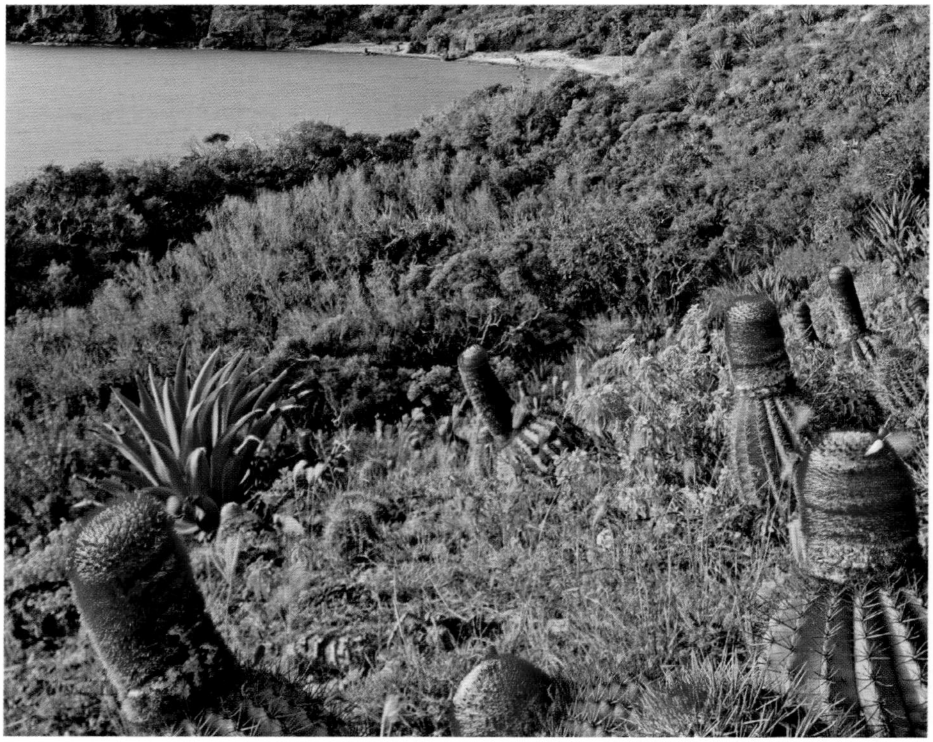

Turk's cap cactuses keep watch over Salt Pond Bay.

POINTS OF INTEREST

FUN FACTS

Sea turtles come to St. John Island's beaches to nest. Several species have been spotted there, including hawksbill, leatherback and green sea turtles.

St. John is a birder's paradise, with more than 144 species spotted throughout the year. According to NPS, the best trail for spotting feathered friends is the Francis Bay Salt Pond Trail.

WORDS TO THE WISE

Driving in the Virgin Islands is different than an American road trip. Why? There, residents drive on the left side of the road! Be sure to follow the correct traffic patterns on your vacation.

There are more than 500 types of fish in the Virgin Islands, but rangers ask that you refrain from feeding any of them. Doing so can disrupt their patterns and make them less friendly to visitors.

We quickly discovered on a drive inland that the residents have adopted many British customs. We also found that picking up hitchhiking locals, especially elders, was not an option—it was mandatory. From that experience we learned about places to see, most of them within the park. Hiking to sugar mills that were abandoned, historical Taino petroglyph rock carvings and subtropical rainforests filled our days.

The Annaberg sugar factory ruins date back to the 1780s, when the island was owned by Denmark, sugar cane was king and more than 300 slaves were used to clear the land, build stone structures and toil in the fields. Terraced hillsides are reminders of plantation farming, but tropical plants that were once cleared for raising cane are now reclaiming the site.

Twenty hiking trails offer short and long ventures to moist high-elevation forests, desert terrain, mangrove swamps and beautiful beaches. The island's highest point and some of the most spectacular views are found on Bordeaux Mountain, which rises to 1,277 feet and plunges dramatically to the sea over a distance of just three-quarters of a mile.

There is much to see in the national park, including more than 50 species of tropical birds and some 800 species of plants like bay rum trees and tropical orchids. But throughout our trek the sea was never far from sight, beckoning to us. A day of sightseeing must be followed by sight-sea-ing along sandy, sun-drenched beaches and pristine, vibrant blue waters.

Larry and I spent most of our time photographing, but at day's end, sunsets were watched, local culinary specialties were consumed and warm breezes lulled us to sleep each night. ■

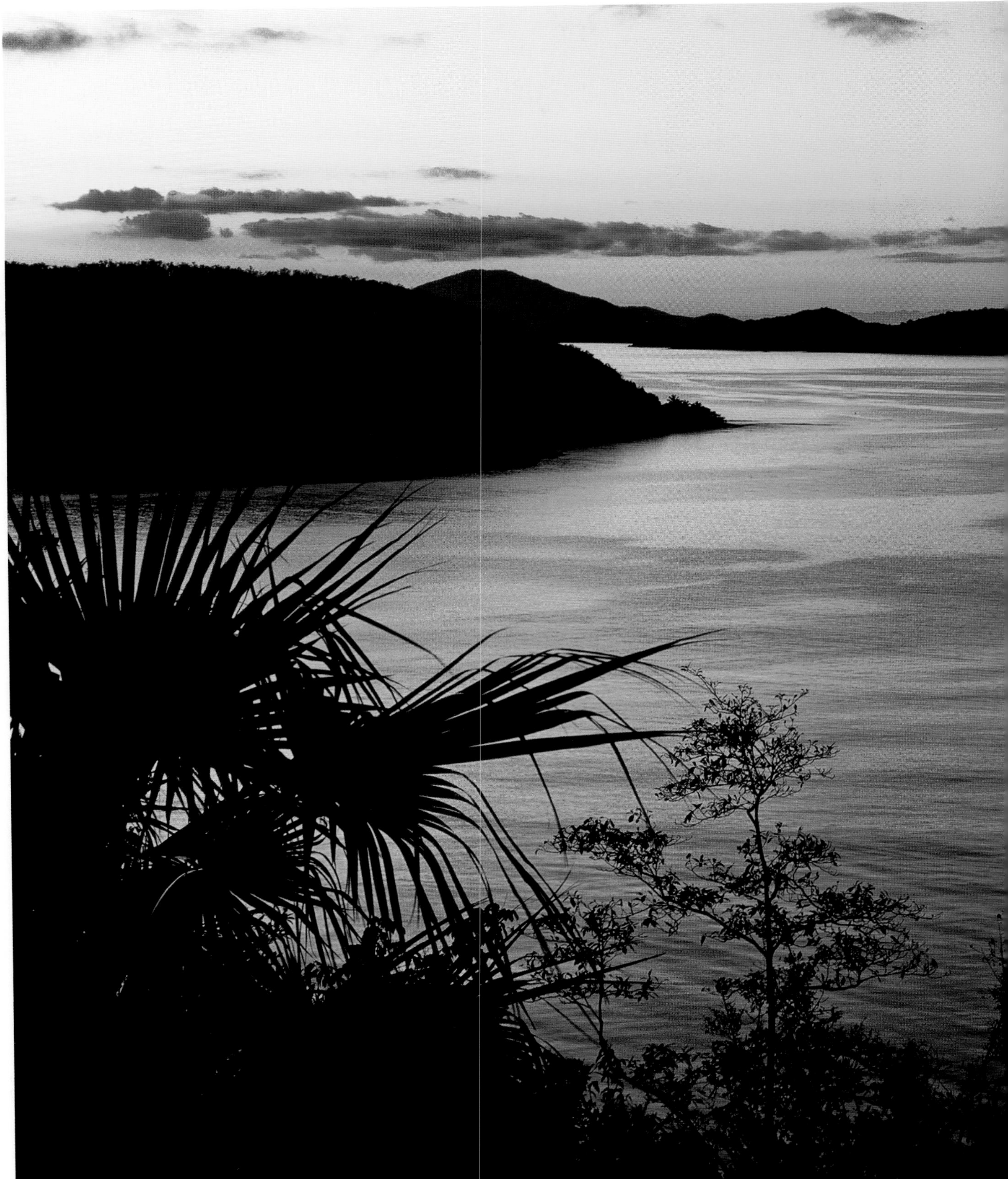

▼
A soothing sunset silhouettes a teyer palm at Cinnamon Bay on the north coast.

EVERGLADES NATIONAL PARK

1920

Even before it was a national park, the Everglades drew many with its natural beauty. At right, Ezra B. Thompson makes movies in the park.

2008

Above, the Everglades still attract creative people who want to preserve the beauty of nature through photography.

THEN: U.S. NATIONAL PARK SERVICE; NOW: PBNJ PRODUCTIONS/GETTY IMAGES